MONEY FOR NOTHING

M. ALLEN HENDERSON

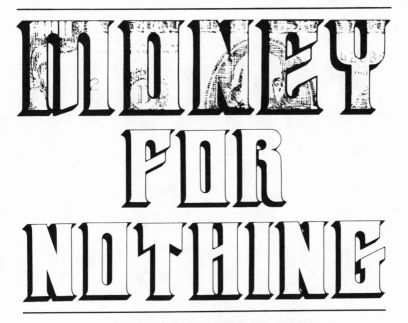

MONEY FOR NOTHING

RIP-OFFS, CONS AND SWINDLES

PALADIN PRESS
BOULDER, COLORADO

Money for Nothing: Rip-offs, Cons and Swindles
by M. Allen Henderson
Copyright © 1986 by Paladin Press

ISBN 0-87364-389-5
Printed in the United States of America

Published by Paladin Press, a division of
Paladin Enterprises, Inc., P.O. Box 1307,
Boulder, Colorado 80306, USA.
(303) 443-7250

Direct inquiries and/or orders to the above address.

Contents

For Mark and Molly, with love

Introduction

*The thing about a con man is, he'd rather make a
little money dishonestly than make a lot of money
doing honest work.*
                                    —Joe Henderson

As Woody Guthrie wrote, "Some men rob you with a six-
gun, some with a fountain pen." The thieves whose exploits
fill the pages of this book are of the latter class, practitioners
of theft by guile. While the confidence artist's trusty pen
is still a must for signing contracts and forging checks, the
modern-day swindler has a greater variety of tools at his
fingertips than did his predecessors in the grift. With the
telephone, computer, sophisticated photocopying equipment, television, and radio to advance his schemes, the professional swindler thrives today as never before. While all
armed robberies in the United States in 1983 accounted for
losses of approximately $500 million, con artists, forgers,
and frauds ripped off more than $50 billion during that year,
according to FBI estimates.

Times change, but the prerequisites of the trade remain
the same as they always have been. To succeed as a confidence artist, one must have a goldbricker's heart, a silver
tongue, and the brass to carry a scam through to the end,
no matter how outrageous it may be.

We have used only stories from current news media in
order to give the reader an accurate picture of some of the
kinds of swindles that are being perpetrated today across
the country. The diversity within this field is enormous.

1

Among the cons and swindles commonly practiced today are investment fraud, pyramid scams, credit-card fraud, counterfeiting, forgery, spiritual bunco, false charity funds, and real estate and loan fraud. Victims of these frauds may be led to believe they will get something for nothing, but the reverse is generally true.

Where do victims of confidence games and swindles meet the crooks who rip them off? Just about anywhere—on the street, on their doorsteps, at church. They may be introduced by mutual friends at business meetings, at the club, by another parent at a PTA meeting, or by their kid's coach at a school soccer match. A swindler may also make contact through the mail or over the telephone, usually offering "the opportunity of a lifetime."

What does the con artist look like? He—or she—may look like a transient, a business executive, a teacher, a drug dealer, a housewife, or a Gypsy. He may use the high-pressure tactics of the old-time snake-oil salesman, or he may impress you as an easygoing kind of guy, as reasonable and low-key as Ward Cleaver.

The con artist may pose quite convincingly as a lawyer, doctor, minister, financial advisor, car dealer, TV or magazine photographer, repairman, policeman, IRS agent, or bank executive. He may also actually be any one of the above.

The question most people ask me is "Who falls for these cons, anyway?" The answer is almost anybody can fall for some type of con—at one time or another. A real confidence *artist* worthy of the title is a powerful persuader. He or she is able to manipulate others by playing on their needs and emotions. Greed can make one vulnerable to a smooth-talking con man, but just as often he will attempt to arouse fear or pity in his victim in order to effect a rip-off.

He's a good actor, or he couldn't run a scam. If he doesn't think his references are good enough, he may dupe a well-respected member of the community into advocating his program. The reader will see how Hollywood celebrities have been conned into lending their names to outright swindles, or have actually had their names stolen in the promotion of a dishonest money-making venture.

The elderly are frequently targets of scams, but the middle-aged and young are conned too. Homeowners, landlords, tenants, housewives, business executives, office workers, pensioners, paupers, even Uncle Sam—all are targets, and sometimes victims, of cons and swindles.

Besieged as we are by the rip-off artist at every turn, how can we hope to avoid his so-called deals? Isn't there any way to avoid being taken?

There's no absolute proof against being fooled, but by learning to recognize the elements of a scam when we encounter one, we can certainly be a lot safer. By reading the stories in this book, some shocking, some amusing, the reader will see patterns emerge, for there are common threads that run through every confidence game. By becoming familiar with the way these games work, nine times out of ten we can intuitively recognize a scam for what it is.

In some cases, names have been changed or withheld by request in order to protect the innocent. Because stories in this book have been taken from current news media, it was not possible to give the outcome in every case. Information in each story is as complete as possible.

In an effort to make this book as up-to-date as possible, intensive research was conducted over a three-month period during the autumn of 1985, at the height of the "confidence season." (Con games and other white-collar crime tend to peak in the fall).

Potpourri

*You know a guy's a con man when you get in about
two in the morning and you see him coming out
of your house with the silverware—and he hits you
up for cab fare home. You know he's a con artist
if you give it to him.*

—Anonymous con man

It may seem inappropriate to use the term *potpourri*, with
its suggestion of sweet-smelling flowers, to describe the
rotten confidence schemes detailed in this chapter. The word
is apt, however, when you consider that its literal meaning
is "rotten pot." The French *pourrir* and the English *putrid*
are descended from the same Latin root.

A *potpourri* is also a miscellany; and within the pages of
this chapter the reader will find a regular hodgepodge of
cons. Some are big-time crimes, others petty grifts. Some
are so low-down that it is difficult to believe that anyone
had the heart—or lack of heart—to pull them off. Others,
however, are amusing in retrospect, even to the occasional
good-natured victim.

The perpetrators of these cons are indeed a motley crew.
Old, middle-aged, and young, they come from all walks of
life, use different MOs, and travel in different crowds. They
do, however, share a few common characteristics: All possess
an extraordinary degree of chutzpah (unmitigated effrontery
or impudence), all are thieves, of one sort or another, and
all are inspired liars.

Hocus-Pocus

Johnny Digiaccomo, a forty-year-old Arizona man, entered the Wolverine saloon, a gay bar in Anchorage, Alaska, shortly after midnight on June 26, 1985. The truth about what happened after that is difficult to unravel from the stories told by Digiaccomo and saloon personnel. Was this man an armed robber posing as a magician, or a well-meaning job-seeker victimized by homosexual harassment?

Chuck and Sharon Sealy, owners of the Wolverine, claim that shortly before closing time Digiaccomo began to practice rope tricks, ostensibly demonstrating a Houdini-style magic act. Sharon Sealy was not impressed when she saw how he had tied up her husband and two young men who had been drinking at the bar. It did not, as she said later at Digiaccomo's trial, look like a magic trick to her.

After he had tied up the men, she said, Digiaccomo held a handgun to her head, and she felt that it was her "last minute." Just then the phone rang, and Chuck Sealy took advantage of the momentary distraction to lunge clumsily at Digiaccomo, who cracked the rope-bound man over the head with his handgun. Everyone in the Wolverine then mobbed Digiaccomo and wrested the weapon from his grasp.

That's the Sealys' story. The following is Johnny Digiaccomo's account, given as testimony at his trial, where he appeared in a wheelchair. The police arrested the wrong man on that June night, he said; he had been the victim of the ruckus, not the instigator. A stranger in the neighborhood, he had gone to the Wolverine in search of part-time work, and had been shocked when the bartender, who was in drag, kissed him on the cheek. Reacting in what he termed "a normal male way," he shoved the bartender as well as Chuck Sealy and then the patrons of the bar piled on top of him and beat him up, hurting his back. He heard some of them say that they would have an orgy with him.

In order to extricate himself from the wormpile, he began to protest that he would sue the Sealys. They then called the police, he said, hoping to preserve their bar and their good name by having him put away on a false charge. He says the owners and employees of the bar are liars.

Digiaccomo was acquitted because the jury members could not agree on a verdict.

Marbles Con Man

South African entrepreneur Ronald Skjoldhammer seemed trustworthy to the London businessmen who took him up on his offer. A well-spoken fellow in his early fifties, he came from a strong church background and belonged to the Salvation Army. Besides, the deal he was offering was impossible for a go-ahead kind of guy to refuse.

He had more than $100 million worth of Angolan diamonds formerly owned by an exiled president stashed away in a safe-deposit box in Amsterdam, he said. For a fraction of that amount he could get his clients a share of the loot.

The businessmen gave him the money he requested, and as security he gave them a worthless postdated check, ownership deeds to two no-account race horses, and a showy but flawed emerald ring.

When, several months later, the diamonds had still not been delivered, his clients grew suspicious and gained a court order to open the safe-deposit box. Instead of diamonds, it contained forty-three glass marbles.

Skjoldhammer was arrested and brought to trial at the Old Bailey in London. He was convicted of six charges of defrauding the businessmen and, in the autumn of 1985, was sentenced to jail for seven years. Skjoldhammer burst into tears when Judge Abdela told him that his "glib persuasiveness" had led to "the most blatant fraud and deception that could have been practiced on anybody."

Diamond Switch

Here he comes, a down-at-the-heels Eastern European. He is of average height, but on the heavy side. His mustache and what little of his hair remains are gray. He tells a sad tale, in excellent Yiddish interpersed with broken English. He has fallen on hard times and is forced to part with a valuable diamond ring. His loss is your gain!

According to Mark Mendelsohn of the Toronto, Canada, police department's ethnic squad, this poor old man is a con artist who works his wiles on Jewish businessmen, especially clothiers. He travels through Canada, saying that he must somehow get to Toronto, and is thus attempting to sell his ring for far less than its real worth. The businessman is led to believe that he can do a good deed for one of his own and make a profit at the same time—a combination few people could refuse.

Two clothiers, one in Regina and one in Sault Ste. Marie, Canada, reportedly fell for the scam, which runs as follows in both instances: The con man explains his pitiable situation and shows the victim a ring. It has a center diamond weighing 4.5 carats, surrounded by twelve smaller diamonds, all set on a gold band. Just to prove his honesty, he tells the victim to take the ring to an appraiser. It is worth about $9,000. The victim pays the con man $4,500 and $500 in merchandise, puts him on a bus, and wishes him Godspeed. When he tries to sell the ring, he discovers that the old geezer has pulled a switch, and he is left holding a worthless but cleverly made piece of costume jewelry. Police say that the fake is impossible to distinguish from the real thing with the naked eye. By the time the clothier realizes that he had been had, the con artist is long gone.

Missing Husband Con

Kenneth Kervin, a man serving time for rape in South Carolina, used prison telephones to blackmail a New York woman whose husband had been reported missing by the news media. Kervin and other inmates invented a story that the missing man was being held hostage by the CIA, and then he conned the desperate woman out of $1,500 "ransom money."

In September 1985, Judge Tom Ervin sentenced twenty-five-year-old Kenneth Kervin to sixteen years for his part in the crime, but only five of those years will be served on top of the twenty-year sentence he is already serving. Kervin pleaded guilty to charges of obtaining money under false pretenses, avoiding payment of telecommunication services, unlawful use of a telephone, and conspiracy in the extortion.

Pet Scam

Scanning the lost-and-found section of the Chicago newspapers, Willie Jones selected missing pet ads from which to cull his victims, according to police. He would call the pet owners and tell them he had found their animals. As the ads contained descriptions of the lost pets, he was able to lie convincingly. He would then instruct the distraught owners to leave a specific amount of money, usually between $50 and $100, in a phone booth near a Trailways bus station. If the owner paid the ransom, Jones said, the animal would be returned. Otherwise Jones threatened to give it to a lab that would use it for scientific experiments.

Michelle Gaspar, of the Anti-Cruelty Society, alerted police to the scam. "This man has a certain meanness that we find intolerable," she said.

Gaspar had attempted to catch the culprit herself by placing three phony ads in Chicago papers, but was unsuccessful. A woman who had lost her Doberman pinscher cooperated with police, however, and her help enabled plainclothes officers to nab Jones in the act of picking up the seventy-dollar bait she had left in the drop area specified by the extortionist. Although she has not yet recovered her dog, she says, she is glad that Jones was brought to justice.

A circuit court jury found Jones guilty on the technical charge of attempted theft and sentenced him on October 18, 1985, to 364 days in jail, the maximum for the offense.

Spin Around the Block

You have to be a better than average car thief to beguile a Rolls Royce owner into handing you the keys to the car. Kathleen Butler, who had never before let anyone, even her grown kids, drive her classic 1968 Rolls, watched an imposter steal the automobile and waved good-bye with a smile.

The truth is, she didn't suspect a thing—at first. A charming, blond man in his early twenties showed up on her doorstep one day to talk about the car. He said that he was Kevin Rice, the son of Jack Rice, a Providence, Rhode Island, auto dealer with whom Ms. Butler was acquainted. Friendly and personable, Kevin told Ms. Butler that his father had told him all about the Rolls, and he had come hoping to get a look at it. He admired the car, worth $50,000, and gave Ms. Butler advice as to its care, cautioning her not to sell it too cheaply. An hour after leaving the premises, he called to ask whether he could take the automobile for a test drive; he thought he would like to buy it, he said.

Ms. Butler agreed to let him take the car for "a spin around the block." It had no license plate, but the young man said that was no problem. He had brought along a plate from his dad's dealership. After putting the plate on the Rolls, he cheerfully motored away. Ms. Butler was not to see her car again for seven weeks.

She grew suspicious long before that, however, calling the dealership four hours after the young man had left. When she asked to speak to Jake Rice's son, Kevin, she was informed that Jake did not have a son.

The Rolls was recovered intact in New Jersey, and police arrested Kevin Jamison in Tavares, Florida, on suspicion of car theft shortly afterward. Jamison, 24, is also alleged to have conned car salesmen into letting him test-drive various valuable automobiles, including a red Corvette, a 1972 Mercedes Convertible, and a $51,000 British-made Lotus. Police say that he simply takes off in the car and does not return. In at least one such case he is alleged to have tried to sell a stolen vehicle to another dealer.

Jamison waived extradition and was returned to Rhode Island, where he has been held on another car-theft charge and for violating parole.

Multi-Talented Impersonator

In 1983, Richard Possemato was discharged from the U.S. Army under less than honorable conditions. In 1984 he was indicted on sixteen charges involving confidence scams, but vanished while awaiting trial. He took advantage of this respite from justice to con more victims so that, when he was arrested and tried in Cambridge, Massachusetts, in 1985, he was charged with twenty-six counts of theft, forgery, and uttering (passing) forged documents. Using the aliases Ricky Marciano, Anthony Sparticino, Ricky Sparticino, Richard Gambino, Richard Demasi, Rick DeMarco, and Ricky Orlandello, the twenty-three-year-old con artist had stolen $26,000 and four cars from nine women and tricked a man out of his car by pretending he was a prospective buyer, according to District Attorney Ralph Martin.

A smooth operator, Possemato preyed on women by playing on their emotions. In some cases he would become intimate with a woman to facilitate ripping her off.

"I make a date with a woman and show up early," Possemato explained to a police officer during the course of one of his arrests. "They are never ready, so while they're in the shower or getting dressed, I go through their pocketbooks."

On one such occasion, on the pretext of giving a woman a ride to the airport, he convinced her to leave her credit card at home so that it would not be stolen when she went to Florida. While she was getting ready for her trip, he stole the card.

On several occasions he stole the cars of his "friends" under the pretext of having the vehicles repaired. Once, while using this gambit under the name of Ricky Orlandello, he called a young woman who had entrusted him with her car. Claiming to be Ricky's brother, he told her that Ricky had been hurt in a crash and might die. When she asked about the car, he berated her for thinking about such a thing when Ricky's life was in danger. Two days later he called back and told her that Ricky was dead. Unfortunately for Possemato, this nice bit of creativity went unrewarded, as he was picked up two days later with the woman's car.

Another favorite game of Possemato's was to get his so-called friends to cash forged and stolen checks for him, and then to entertain them with the money. They found out too late that they had been suckered into hanging paper for Possemato, and that they would be held legally responsible for making good on the bad checks.

Possemato told a young lady whose Datsun 280ZX he coveted that he was the Kamikaze Kid, a kick boxer from Atlantic City. He wound up stealing the car, and was motoring along minding his own business when he spied a Corvette he liked better. As luck would have it, the 'vette's driver was a young woman. He followed her to the Ramada Inn in Woburn, Massachusetts, and saw her sit down with two men in the lounge. When she left for a moment, Possemato swaggered into the lounge and attempted to run off the two men.

"That's my girl you're messing with," he said.

The men backed off immediately, telling Possemato they didn't want any trouble. Possemato, making a tremendous error in judgment, now threatened them with the inside of a jail if they didn't get lost. One of the men asked whether he was a police officer.

"Damn right, I'm a state cop," Possemato answered.

The two men just so happened to be a state trooper and a Woburn police officer. They knew who Possemato was because they had both received official information on him the day before, and arrested him on the spot for impersonating a police officer.

For his string of cons, including theft, forgery, and passing forged documents, Possemato has been sentenced to six to ten years in the Massachusetts Correctional Institution at Cedar Junction.

Willing Benefactress

Eighty-one-year-old Sarah Brooks met Phil Dwight, a gas station attendant fifty years her junior, near the retirement village where she lived in Florida's Hillsborough County. This was August 1982; Dwight was pumping gas. After his fateful meeting with Mrs. Brooks, he didn't have to pump gas anymore.

"She just took a liking to him, and he moved on it," a Hillsborough Sheriff's Department investigator later said.

Dwight liked to cruise around in Mrs. Brooks' Cadillac, and she was happy to let him borrow it. On two occasions he asked her for money to pay for damages to other automobiles he said he had run into, and both times she paid. Another time she gave him cash to cover the medical expenses of a child he said he had accidently injured in a crash while he was driving the Cadillac.

Mrs. Brooks also handed over money to a friend of Dwight's in order, as he allegedly told her, to ransom Dwight from a gang of kidnappers. The friend told the elderly woman that he was acting on Dwight's instructions, according to police officials.

Mrs. Brooks' relatives suspected that something was amiss when she began to ask them for money. When they questioned her about where her savings had gone, she explained about Phil Dwight, and how he just kept having these terrible things happen to him. Of course, she said, she had helped him out. Her family, unable to convince her that her young friend was cheating her, called in the police.

On August 30, 1984, an investigation was launched, and authorities discovered that, over a two-year period, Mrs. Brooks had written numerous checks to Dwight totaling $250,000. This amount did not include the car-repair payments, medical expenses, or ransom money, for which no records have been found. Authorities could find no evidence that the Cadillac had ever been in a collision.

Dwight was arrested without incident as he left his Apollo Beach home one afternoon, and police moved quickly to freeze possible accounts in Dwight's name at twenty

Hillsborough banks in hopes of recovering any money he might have stashed away. At one bank, records showed about $89,000 in deposits written to Dwight from Sarah Brooks.

Although Dwight had not been flush before meeting his benefactress and had not held a steady job for two years after befriending her, authorities allege that during the time he knew Mrs. Brooks he acquired the house in Apollo Beach, a new Pontiac Trans Am, a thirty-foot cabin cruiser, a speed boat, and a new four-wheel-drive truck.

Dwight has been charged with grand theft.

Hard-Luck Story Peddler

He'd make a super salesman and a terrific actor, according to reports. And, in a sense, he has earned his living by practicing both professions, for twenty-five-year-old Jimmy Franklin is a con artist. He is so good at what he does—peddling hard-luck stories for substantial handouts—that some of his victims cannot even bring themselves to be angry with him. They just feel embarrassed and amused.

"If I owned a company that needed a good salesman, I'd go down to the jail and bail him out myself," said the manager of a Shell service station, who gave Franklin eleven dollars in cash and five dollars' worth of gasoline. He hadn't thought to doubt Franklin until he found that two of his employees had also given the man money—on the basis of a different hard-luck story!

"He was so slick, it's hard to be angry," said another of his victims, a woman who gave him $21.

Orange County, Florida, deputy sheriffs figure that more than 200 people gave Franklin about $10,000 before his arrest cut short his yarn-spinning spree; before he was picked up during the summer of 1985, they say, he was "all over the place."

The story he used most often went basically as follows: His wife was having a miscarriage. He was afraid because she was bleeding internally and in pain, but hospital personnel refused to admit her because the young couple did not have enough cash. A young black woman often sat in his car, her head thrown back against the car seat as if she were in pain.

Franklin was good at weaving his surroundings into his stories in order to give himself credibility. Once, pointing to a black family that was moving into a house down the street, he told a bystander that he was moving in and then hit him up for money. Sometimes he would case an apartment complex and say that he was from, for example, apartment 101, so that his tale would sound more realistic.

If a victim had been particularly sympathetic or generous, Franklin would return to collect more money to cover various new medical complications he had invented for his fictitious wife.

If it weren't for John Klingman, a computer salesman, Franklin might still be at large. At about nine o'clock one Sunday morning, Klingman answered a knock at his apartment door, and there stood a very worried-looking young man dressed in a T-shirt and jogging shorts. It was Franklin, but he identified himself as Mark Williams; he asked whether Bob, John Klingman's son, was at home.

When Klingman said that Bob was away at college, the young man seemed desperate. Breathlessly, he said that his pregnant wife needed dialysis treatment and that Bob had promised to help him out. He asked to borrow thirty-four dollars to have his wife admitted to the hospital.

Klingman told him to come back in fifteen minutes. Franklin left, and Klingman was on the way to the automatic teller at his bank to withdraw money when the phone rang. It was a friend of John Klingman's, and when Klingman explained about Mark's frantic state, she told him to call the police because she had heard about the scam on the news. Klingman called the police and left the apartment; Franklin was arrested as he returned for the money.

Klingman later told the police that Franklin seemed like an intelligent well-spoken young man; therefore, Klingman felt it was worth the risk to play the Good Samaritan when Franklin told him he was afraid of losing his baby.

"I sure didn't want that on my conscience," Klingman said.

When asked why he had conned so many people out of their money, Franklin said that he had a $500-a-day cocaine habit. He has been charged with four counts of theft by grand fraud, grand theft of an automobile, and scheming to defraud. (Grand theft by fraud applies to cases in which more than $100 is taken fraudulently from a victim; scheming to defraud applies to cases in which more than ten people are cheated out of money.)

Family Scamming

The tale of the Dullen family is sad indeed, and they have been telling it to anybody who'll listen. They say that they are a poor but (relatively) honest family, victims of a terrible misunderstanding. Out of desperation, they say, Carl Dullen stole some jewelry to provide for his children. Shortly after his arrest for the theft, the family car was ransacked and all of their belongings stolen. Carl Dullen served about six months in jail for stealing the jewelry; this was the first and only time he was convicted of a felony.

In Dullen's own words: "I'm not going to pretend that I am a faultless man, but this whole thing has been blown out of proportion. I have never been a con man, like everyone is saying I am. I don't plan to be a con man in the future. I've never asked anyone to give me money, I can tell you that right now."

He says that police persecute him and his wife, Eva, so unmercifully that they are unable to find work, even at the most menial level. The crowning injustice is the removal of their children, ages four, six, and eight, to foster homes.

"We are a close-knit family," Dullen says, "and the children have always taken part in everything we do. And getting back to the money—if people have given us so darn much of it, how come I've got holes in my shoes? How come we only have the clothes on our backs?"

Beats us, say law-enforcement officials, but the jewel theft charge for which Dullen served time was only the latest in a long career of offenses which they claim are becoming progressively more serious.

Court records show that Carl Dullen spent about four years in county jails and the California Youth Authority between 1964 and 1976 for six incidents involving forgery, exhibiting firearms, possession of stolen property, drunk driving, petty theft, and second degree burglary. He was examined for possible placement in a narcotics rehabilitation facility and committed to the Discovery program for heroin addicts in 1973, but he did not complete the program.

The Dullens, police say, have often used their children and their down-and-out condition to elicit sympathy from potential victims in Oregon and California. Many people have given the family food, clothing, money, and shelter, only to have their belongings stolen the moment their backs are turned.

Court records reveal that the pastor of a Lutheran church filed a complaint against the Dullens, claiming that the family came to him to ask for financial aid. He left the room for a minute, and when he returned the Dullens were gone—along with his ecumenical ring.

In October 1984, a Concord, California, minister reported that the Dullens had stolen about $500 worth of jewelry from his home after he had taken them in, fed and clothed them, and given them $25. The minister said that Carl and Eva Dullen told him they were traveling from Oregon to California and had stopped along the way to visit a friend who had suffered a heart attack. After leaving their friend, they became involved in a car accident and had to spend all their money on hospital bills.

A former landlord of the Dullens maintains that the couple rented a furnished apartment from him and then sold its contents at a garage sale before moving out (all they allegedly left behind was used drug paraphernalia). To make matters worse, the landlord says, he is now being sued by a woman who gave the Dullens a down payment to hold certain items for her. They sold the items to someone else, according to allegations, and kept her payment. The woman holds the landlord responsible and has brought suit against him for breach of promise. The Dullens deny all of the landlord's allegations.

After serving time for the jewel theft conviction, Carl Dullen was given three years' probation, but did not make his probation appointments, according to police. He was arrested in the parking lot of a McDonald's restaurant on an outstanding warrant. A McDonald's employee had called the police, but not because she had any idea that Dullen was wanted by the law. She said that she was upset because Carl struck his daughter while Eva tried to burn one of the other children with a cigarette.

That's not the whole saga, but it's enough to give you a pretty good idea of the kind of bad-mouthing and persecution the Dullens are up against. And, as if life hadn't already been hard enough on Carl and Eva, they say that now that their kids are in protective custody, Eva won't be receiving her usual welfare check. She says she won't be able to pay her rent this month.

Considering the circumstances, I'm betting her present landlord will let it slide. He'll probably consider himself lucky if she doesn't hold a garage sale.

Moving-Day Fiasco

A woman rented a house in Pensacola, Florida, recently, then placed a house-for-rent ad in a local paper and accepted down payments from couples who responded. The woman, known to authorities only by a pseudonym, left the vicinity $3,000 richer before the resultant moving-day fiasco.

None of the would-be tenants suspected that they had been the victims of a scam until the following weekend, when the con woman had told them carpeting, cleaning, and painting would be completed. All had keys to the house, and one couple had already moved a few belongings into the garage. It is interesting to imagine the scene that ensued when the tenants realized what had happened. Each couple had put down two months' rent in advance, in exchange for worthless receipts.

Work in Tropics, Get Iced

Was Howard Crawford a con man, as police investigators claim, a paranoid schizophrenic and borderline mental deficient, as he was diagnosed by court-appointed psychiatrists, or, as his former wife summed him up, simply a man who "had trouble telling the truth?"

Whatever his motivations may have been, the crowds that came to hear him speak in motel conference rooms across the country seemed to love him. A self-styled "simple country boy," he told the unemployed rural job-seekers that his company, TransWorld Careers, would find them lucrative positions overseas in fields from oil refining to highway construction. For a one-time membership fee, which ranged from $350 to $750, he said that TransWorld would seek to place clients in jobs that paid annual, tax-free salaries of $45,000 to $65,000. Employees would also receive a housing allowance, two weeks vacation every four months, and a bonus upon completion of the job, according to his advertising pitch.

"If I feel I can't help a man," Crawford would tell the audience in his good-old-boy drawl, "I'm not going to take his money."

Yet, through TransWorld Careers, a business operated out of his Jacksonville, Florida, apartment by himself and two secretaries, Crawford raked in an estimated $500,000 without ever landing one of his 800 clients a job.

Crawford claimed to have been awarded two Purple Hearts, the Silver Star, Bronze Star, Navy Flying Cross and Medal of Valor while in the U.S. Navy. In fact, he was discharged after serving two months when Navy officials found that he had falsified his application.

He said that he attended Memphis State University, but, if this is true, the university must have lost his records, as they have no evidence of his enrollment.

Crawford's résumé states that he held top management positions in overseas companies, and that he was entertained by the Shah of Iran and the king of Saudi Arabia, but police say that the companies he mentions probably never existed except in Crawford's imagination.

Until the age of forty, in fact, Crawford had merely gone from job to job, without finding anything that he could stick with. He left his wife and remarried—without benefit of divorce—and then, in 1982, he started TransWorld Careers.

Crawford traveled to Colombia, Venezuela, Trinidad, and South Africa between September 1983 and February 1985. He also took clients to Lima, Peru, where he convinced them positions were available with Alpine International, a phony company he himself had set up.

In late 1983 the Georgia Bureau of Investigation (GBI) was alerted by an employee of Brigade Quartermasters, a Marietta, Georgia, survivalist supply store, who said that Crawford had called him asking to hire a hit man. The GBI investigation into the matter was shelved, though, because Crawford did not follow up on the request. In early 1984, Crawford again was reported to the GBI for seeking to hire a hit man, this time by the Sonics Training Facility, a mercenary training school near Atlanta. A meeting was set up in Jacksonville between Crawford, the informant, and an undercover detective with the local sheriff's office who posed as the hit man. The supposed hit man was introduced by the Sonics Facility informant as a former mercenary who had spent time in Thailand.

Crawford said that he had twenty-nine clients who were causing him trouble; he proposed setting up a phony Alpine International office in Bangkok, Thailand, and luring the troublemakers there with the promise of high-salary positions. Then, he said, the hit man should arrange for them to be gathered together on a bus or boat excursion and have them all blown up in an explosion rigged to look like an accident. The clients, Crawford said, should first have time to send postcards and letters home in order to make the operation appear legitimate. He promised to pay $500 a head for each client killed.

The informant and the undercover man agreed, and scheduled a second meeting with Crawford for the following day. At this meeting Crawford gave them his hit list and $1,100 to cover explosives and other expenses, stressing that he wanted no bodies found. The two men left, and a few minutes later GBI officials arrested Crawford.

In September 1985 Crawford pleaded guilty to charges of organized fraud and conspiracy to commit murder, and was sentenced to twelve years in prison.

Was Crawford merely a crook, or was he deranged enough to believe his own stories? No one knows for certain, but while in jail awaiting trial he still clung to his role as head of TransWorld Careers. Seeking to borrow money for legal expenses from a former client, Crawford promised that in exchange for the money he would land him a good job overseas.

Corruption of Operation Airlift

In February of 1982 Hilmer Sandini, then 57, convicted con man and drug smuggler, approached the FBI with a proposition. In return for knocking a few years off his fifteen-year prison sentence for running marijuana, he offered to use his underworld contacts to help the Bureau capture cocaine smugglers and other important traffickers in the trade. FBI officials in Washington, D.C., took him up on the deal and assigned agent Daniel Mitrione to act as his partner.

In March 1985, Mitrione pleaded guilty before a federal grand jury to charges of bribery, conspiracy, and possession of cocaine with intent to distribute. At this writing he is awaiting sentencing, and the outcome of Sandini's trial is not yet known. The story that unfolded during the trials of Mitrione and his partner sounds like the plot of a fast-paced television adventure. Operation Airlift ended in Mitrione's moral and professional downfall. As we shall see, he was subjected to great temptation, and Sandini was expert at playing on his hopes, fears, and desires.

Sandini has been described by Mitrione as a man with a powerful personality, the kind of man that people play up to and seek to impress. Sandini encouraged this tendency in others and benefited from it, according to Mitrione.

In the early days of Operation Airlift, the two partners established an electronic scanning company as a cover. Operating out of Fort Lauderdale Executive Airport, the company offered debugging services in order to lure drug runners into the clutches of the FBI. Sandini and Mitrione assumed that such services would naturally be sought out by smugglers using the airport, and their assumption proved correct. While using the cover the two actually removed police listening devices from drug traffickers' homes, cars, and planes and offered to transport cocaine from South America for them.

Mitrione had great hopes for Operation Airlift's first sting operation, a 2,000-kilo cocaine deal from Paraguay. He would purposely allow the first 1,000-kilo shipment to "walk" into the United States, and take down the names of the buyers. After having bought and resold this shipment without any trouble, the buyers would be lulled into a false sense of security, and so could be easily arrested when they came to pick up a second shipment. Mitrione considered the plan to be a good setup; but it was cancelled at the last minute by Justice Department officials, who refused to allow the first shipment to enter the United States.

"It was at this point that Dan [Mitrione] really changed," observed Sandini in a court statement. "He had severe moods of depression and cursed Washington for having people making decisions that knew absolutely nothing about working under cover. . . . He had better things to do and he wanted in on the big money. And, upon completion of Airlift, he wanted out of the Bureau."

Mitrione also attributed his changed attitude toward the FBI to the frustration he felt at this time.

Mitrione began to observe Sandini's dealings with cocaine smugglers, but did not report them. He wanted to allow the business to continue in order to get information on the people he was observing. He knew that Sandini was still involved with the drug world for profit, but saw no way to stop him without scrapping the operation. Mitrione saw a lot of cocaine walk into the country without interference, and realized that, by not having the shipments busted, he was going against official policy, and thus making himself vulnerable to possible blackmail attempts by Sandini. Mitrione knew that it was very unlikely that the Justice Department would ever sanction the walking of drugs by FBI Miami.

Mitrione said that he sampled cocaine only once, and that the incident was unavoidable. He and Sandini had flown into Pittsburgh, Pennsylvania, to meet organized crime figures involved in drug running. During the meeting, he was forced to snort cocaine in order to show that he was not a law enforcement officer. He did not tell the FBI about this one-time drug use.

In December, Mitrione threw a party for drug-running pilots, and, on the advice of Sandini, paid for the services of six prostitutes as part of the entertainment. Sandini encouraged Mitrione's gradual break with the Bureau by leading him farther and farther from the straight and narrow. He gave Mitrione a Christmas gift of $3,500 and a $9,000 Rolex watch. Mitrione accepted both, although he believed the money to have come from drug sales.

"I had been totally compromised by Sandini, and he was well aware of it," Mitrione said in court statements. "I lost leverage with Sandini, and he gained control of the situation."

Mitrione frequently accepted large cash payments from his partner after this. These payments, along with the $250,000 that he embezzled from the FBI, allowed him to buy a $12,000 car, a $35,000 boat, twenty bars of silver, a house, and property in Fort Myers. He also spent $25,000 for a gambling spree in Atlantic City and the Bahamas, and $75,000 for entertaining. He lent $45,000 to friends and kept $200,000 in a suitcase.

Mitrione had heard about complaints at the Bureau about Operation Airlift; FBI officials were wondering why no cocaine had been seized. When, in March 1983, Mitrione and Sandini learned of a shipment that had been stranded in Memphis, Tennessee, Sandini conceived of a plan whereby they could keep the feds happy, keep Operation Airlift going, and profit from the situation, all at the same time.

They would take the shipment, skim off 42 kilos for later sale, and then turn in 200 kilos to the FBI in Washington.

The stranded cocaine was in a pickup truck in the parking lot of a Sheraton hotel in Memphis. Mitrione unloaded 42 one-kilo bags and packed them into three suitcases, which he placed in Sandini's rental car. Then he drove the truck to the parking lot of a grocery store in Fort Lauderdale where, by prior arrangement with FBI Miami, local police picked up the remaining 200 kilos. Sandini made about $1.6 million from the sale of the 42 kilos of cocaine, according to Mitrione.

"I was deep into it all. . .caught up in it all, and had made the leap across the line ethically," Mitrione later testified when asked why he had gone along with the plan. He was also afraid of being compromised by his partner if he refused to participate.

"Sandini," he stated, "already had me in several situations, receipt of money, allowances of cocaine to go through traffic, receipt of gifts."

In the spring of 1983 the FBI ended Operation Airlift, and Mitrione eventually admitted that he had destroyed evidence, allowed huge shipments of cocaine to enter the country untouched, ingested cocaine, hired prostitutes for parties, embezzled $250,000 in government funds, and taken $850,000 from the unreported sale of cocaine shipments.

Trust Betrayed: Two Stories

At 97, Minnie Swanson has brought to justice the man who swindled her out of her estate. Her gumption paid off, too—judges have awarded her settlements of more than $2 million, more than doubling the amount of money that was stolen from her.

She and her brother, the late Arthur Metcalf, gave power of attorney to Robert Jackman so that he could manage their funds for them. They thought that it would be easier to hire someone to pay their health, nursing, and living expenses than to do it themselves.

In late 1980, Arthur Metcalf died, and Jackman began to divert the funds to his own use. Much of the $900,000 estate was apparently spent in entertaining potential investors in Intersea Fisheries, Jackman's company. According to Craig R. McLellan, Ms. Swanson's lawyer, Jackman said that the company operated in San Diego as well as in the Cayman Islands, but nobody has ever discovered its whereabouts. A year and a half after Metcalf's death, all of the money was gone; like Intersea Fisheries, it has never been found.

Minnie Swanson was not one to stand for this. She sued Jackman and his lawyer for fraud. After a three-week trial, the lawyer's insurance company was ordered to pay her a cool million dollars.

When the insurance company did not pay promptly, Swanson and McLellan sued it, and Swanson was awarded another $800,000. They then sued Swanson's bank for failing to advise her that Jackman was suspected by bank officials of using her money in his own account. In this suit she was awarded $150,000. It just goes to show what can be gained by spirit and a good lawyer.

*　　*　　*

Mary K. Appley, 37, thought she had a good lawyer in an old family friend, Stuart West. Unfortunately, she was mistaken.

Mary has multiple sclerosis. Before her father, Emil Kochton, died in 1971, West promised him that he would take care of the young woman, and the lawyer eventually became the sole trustee of Mary Appley's $950,000 trust fund.

Far from fulfilling his promise to his friend, however, West began to embezzle money from Appley's investment account, and led her into investment scams, even getting her to obtain $45,000 from her mother "to keep her investments going," according to U.S. Attorney Howard Pearl.

Pearl described West as a chronic gambler who owed $139,500 to Caesar's Palace, the Tropicana, and other Las

Vegas casinos in 1983—three times his adjusted gross income, as shown on his tax returns for that period.

Appley is now financially dependent on her mother. Herself the mother of a fifteen-year-old girl, she receives no alimony or child support from her daughter's father, who left her when the child was a year old.

According to Pearl, losing her trust fund meant the loss of her independence and made it impossible for Appley to have a house with such conveniences as ramps for her wheelchair.

West pleaded guilty, and said that he was sorry.

He was sentenced to seven years in prison, followed by five years' probation; he was also ordered to make restitution, although he still has gambling debts.

A Pack of Poseurs

During the Eighties, imposters cropped up all over the country, pretending to be cowboys, policemen, doctors, lawyers, government officials, nuns, and heaven knows what-all. Here are a few examples.

- A church in Norristown, Pennsylvania, put out an alert in its Sunday bulletin that parishioners should be on the lookout for two women posing as nuns. There had been complaints from local businesses that two nuns had been walking in and harassing people for donations. The women failed to show any identification, or to say where the donations would go.

- A man posing as an author and restaurant critic got himself a free summer vacation in the Northern Rockies, mooching rides, rooms, and meals through Montana, Idaho, and British Columbia. He owes thousands of dollars to three women he hired as assistants to drive him around and act as his press agents. He hired the women one after the other, as they each found they couldn't get along with him.

"He's a real pusher, and he'd go way, way, out of his

way to get free lodging and food," said one of the women.

Photographers in Billings, Montana, and Colorado Springs and Denver, Colorado, also say that he owes them money for photographs they took for his restaurant book. In some cases, after eating free in restaurants, he borrowed money from owners for deposits on books he said he would forward to them containing critiques of their eateries.

Police would like to ask the would-be writer some questions, but they can't find him.

- In January 1985, Clair Morrison and her brothers, Joseph and Dennis Imbesi, were conned in a hospital waiting room by a man pretending to be a doctor.

As the three anxiously waited for news of their father after his heart surgery, a stocky, well-dressed man with dark, curly hair entered the room and began to use the telephone. Introducing himself as "Dr. Ross," he apparently spoke to personnel at other hospitals, inquiring after patients and giving prescriptions for drugs to be administered to them.

Joseph Imbesi, thinking that "Dr. Ross" was a cardiologist, began asking him questions about heart surgery. The supposed doctor was friendly and helpful; when the family needed to leave the room for a few minutes, he even offered to watch their belongings for them.

When the three returned, however, Ms. Morrison's purse was gone, and so was the man whom they had assumed to be a kindly physician. The purse contained $100 in cash and the elder Mr. Imbesi's gold watch. The watch had been appraised at about $1,300, but its sentimental value made it priceless to Ms. Morrison.

A few hours after the theft was reported, hospital security personnel received a call from a man who identified himself as "Detective Rogers" from the Baltimore Police Department. A black male had been arrested with Ms. Morrison's purse, he said. The next day, "Officer Davis" called to confirm the arrest.

Investigators assigned to the case believed that the arrest story was merely a red herring. For one thing, there was no Detective Rogers or Officer Davis on the police force. Furthermore, the description of "Dr. Ross" fit a wily con artist named Joseph Tito Statchuk who had been convicted several times on charges of impersonating a lawyer. (By the way, Statchuk is white.)

Statchuk had earned himself quite a reputation at the local courthouse for his escapades over a ten-year period. In one case, he was sentenced to five years in prison for collecting $2,750 from clients who thought that he was a lawyer. One woman hired him to represent her son on murder charges; this woman's neighbor then enlisted his services to get *her* son released early from prison so that he could attend her husband's funeral service.

In another case, Statchuk was hired to teach hotel employees how to spot thieves. He was later convicted of theft for burglarizing the hotel that he worked for, and sentenced to several months in a Washington, D.C., prison.

When Statchuk, alias Dr. Ross, learned that he was under suspicion for stealing Ms. Morrison's purse from the waiting room, he mailed her father's watch to her home.

He was brought to trial for the purse theft in late October 1985, appearing before Judge Patricia S. Pytash. She was not amused by his tricks.

"Do you know what upsets me about this?" asked the judge before sentencing.

". . . [That it happened] in the intensive care unit, where someone is distraught and upset because their parent is in there and they don't know what the outcome will be. At the worst time in their life, someone does something like this to them."

Joseph S. Lyons, the attorney for the defense, spoke of Statchuk's medical condition—ironically, the impersonator himself has heart trouble—and of his deep involvement with religious activities as business manager of the Word of Faith Cathedral. Lyons also pointed out that Statchuk had returned the watch to Clair Morrison.

The judge, apparently unmoved by these considerations, said that Statchuk had a four-page record of "nothing but fraud"; she found the defendant guilty of theft and sentenced him to eighteen months in prison, the maximum term for the offense.

According to the prosecutor, State's Attorney Haven Kodeck, Statchuk is an interesting guy.

"I think Joe enjoys the chase more than the actual accomplishment of the crime," Kodeck said.

According to Robert Wolf, a lawyer who represented Statchuk in an impersonation case several years earlier, "If he [Statchuk] had channeled that energy somewhere else, he could probably have been a neuro-surgeon. He appeared to be very bright."

*   *   *

Other favorite poses of con artists in recent years have been police officers, lawyers, IRS and Social Security collection agents, photographers, and Red Cross workers. (Before letting strangers in your house, be sure to thoroughly check their ID!)

Common Bunco

They (home repair swindlers) are not all Gypsies. Some are white trash Anglos—lowlife salamanders.
—Tony Perales, San Antonio Police Bunco Unit detective

In office buildings and exclusive clubs around the country, wheeler-dealers and big-time scammers are inventing ingenious new ways to rip off the general public—and each other. Meanwhile, their less sophisticated bunco brethren are out on the streets running the same old moth-eaten scams they have always run—with considerable success.

The most common of these old-time scams are home-repair swindles, the pigeon drop and bank examiner schemes, and the Jamaican hustle. Money-changing schemes, betting ruses, three-card monte, and other classics are also still practiced around the country. These are generic cons, suitable for everyday use, but nothing fancy. The most amazing thing about them is that they work at all, since none of the schemes sounds particularly clever when you hear about it after the fact. This is because outlining the elements of a con is like telling the plot of a good movie; it gives the listener no idea of the power of the performance. The success of a con man, like that of an actor, lies in his ability to put on a convincing show.

People of all ages are taken in by common bunco, but the elderly are the most vulnerable and the most frequently targeted by flimflammers.

The pigeon drop, bank examiner scheme, and Jamaican

hustle are all cons that generally involve putting the mark on the send—in other words, getting him to withdraw money from a bank account. In some instances, when the crooks know that an intended victim is carrying cash, the send is eliminated.

In the pigeon drop, two people, often women, generally work together to cheat the victim, usually an elderly woman. One of the accomplices says that she has found a large amount of money and asks the intended victim what to do with it. A note is often stashed with the money; it is intended to soothe any guilt feelings the mark may have about keeping money that belongs to someone else. (Such notes tend to be none too subtle. Three examples, from actual pigeon-drop scams in Illinois, Georgia, and New York, read as follows: "Will be deposited for kilos;" "Sal—This money was won at the race track. The IRS is after me. See you in Switzerland, your brother, Manny;" and "Here's another $45,000 from Sunday night's job. Get it to Ira right away. He's leaving tonight.")

Meanwhile, the other partner, who pretends not to know the woman who has supposedly found the money, happens along and gets involved. She says that she works for a lawyer (or some other worldly-wise man) and goes away "to ask him what to do." When she returns, she says that all three women are to take money out of the bank to show good faith and allow the lawyer to hold it for them for a few days until the found money can be legally distributed among them. Or she says that they can divide the money immediately, but each must pay a certain percentage to the IRS. The two con women leave, taking the victim's savings. If she has received a share of the money that was purportedly found, she will discover that a switch was made and she will be left holding a bag full of cut-up newspaper or play money.

In the bank examiner scheme, the victim receives a phone call from someone who claims to be a police officer or an officer at her bank. He says that a teller is suspected of stealing from people's savings accounts, and asks for help in apprehending the felon. The victim should withdraw a certain amount of money from her account, he says; sometimes he requests that she wear gloves, so as not to leave fingerprints on the bills. Later on he will send the police to pick up the money, or else he will collect it himself. After the bills have been carefully scrutinized, the money will be returned to her account. This con works best on elderly women who have a great deal of respect for authority. It is sometimes foiled by inquisitive bank tellers who ask why a customer is withdrawing such a lot of cash. For this reason, a con artist will often tell his vicitm not to tell anyone about the "investigation" until after the "thief" has been caught.

The Jamaican hustle has many variations. In all of these, the victim, usually a man, is treated to some long, confusing cock-and-bull story and eventually asked to hold a roll of bills for a foreigner or out-of-towner who doesn't know his way around. The victim is then asked to give the "foreigner" some of his money—a much smaller amount—to show that he isn't going to take off with the bankroll. The con artist leaves, supposedly to conduct some business, after arranging to meet up again with the mark at a certain time and place. He never returns; and when the victim inspects the bankroll, he discovers that a switch has been made. He is holding newspaper strips instead of greenbacks. Sometimes the victim mistakenly imagines up until this moment that he has in actuality cheated the "Jamaican"; in other cases, he has merely been trying to help a stranger.

In many cities, confidence games are seasonal. Police in Detroit and Pontiac, Michigan, have been trying for years to catch up with a pack of migratory con artists from Alabama and other Southern states who for years have chosen to summer in the Detroit area.

"They come normally in the warm months, flocking in like Gypsies, and then return home when the weather begins to cool. We refer to them as 'The Corporation,'" said Pontiac detective Gary Kraft in an interview with the *Oakland Press,* a local newspaper.

According to Kraft, the Corporation's method of operation is to hang around Social Security offices and check-cashing businesses in order to be sure that their marks would have money in their pockets. In cons that require working in teams, the con men would change partners frequently in order to avoid being identified as confederates. Another trade mark of the Corporation is its use of red and blue bandannas in handkerchief switch schemes.

"When the victim opened the bandanna, all he'd find was newspapers," Kraft said. "Men tend to be victimized more than women, but we had one woman who held onto the handkerchief for days and days before she brought it in. We could tell it hadn't been opened, because the Corporation uses a very precise knot."

A police crackdown on bunco by several cooperating police departments in the area has cut down on the Corporation's summer visits, but few of the ring members have been brought to justice.

"As sure as the thoroughbreds return to Keeneland each fall, so do the con artists," reports Valarie Honeycutt of the Lexington, Kentucky, *Herald-Leader*.

Every year incidences of confidence games peak just as the racing season begins. The con artists are not horse owners or horse racers, according to police, but merely scammers who take advantage of the festive mood of racing season. When excitement is running high and gambling is the order of the day, when Lexington is packed with tourists, all of them using charge cards and flashing cash— that's the perfect time for a con man to visit beautiful Kentucky.

Lexington police say that the bunco artists who descend upon the city typically engage in quick-change scams, plastic crime, and such classic cons as the bank examiner, the Jamaican hustle, and the pigeon drop.

Home-repair fraud is most common all over the nation in autumn, when people are concerned about preparing their homes for the coming cold, snowy, and rainy weather. This is the season when home owners see the handymen roll up in their pickups to offer roofing, asphalting, insulation, chimney repair, painting, and furnace inspection—all at prices that sound too good to be true. Usually they will tell you that they have done a job in the neighborhood and still have some materials left over that they want to use up. The contractor who appears, unbidden, at your door—or, more likely, in your yard, where you are out raking leaves— is not the man with whom to do business. Find a reputable person in your own community who has references from people you know.

The bunco repairman or contractor ends up charging more than he should, even if he had done a good job. After he leaves, the homeowner discovers that the job is not finished or not even begun, or that the situation is worse than before ("weatherproofing" on a leaky roof runs in the first rain, ruining the lawn around the house, for example.)

The furnace inspector tells you that he is from the utility company, or that, if he doesn't inspect your furnace right away, you will forfeit the warranty. In any case, he says that the inspection is free. Once inside, he pretends to look over your heating system, then tries to scare you by telling you the furnace is leaking carbon monoxide, is just about to blow up, or some other such malarkey. He will also offer you the opportunity to buy a new furnace, or to enlist his services to fix your old model.

Utility companies don't send servicemen around to check furnaces door-to-door. If you're in doubt, ask the "serviceman" to wait while you call the company. And look up the number in the phone book, don't use one he gives you! He may have an accomplice waiting by the phone.

Con artists of all descriptions swarm like vultures to scenes of disaster. Beware of self-styled fix-it men who arrive at your doorstep after a flood, hurricane, tornado, or wind storm. Bunco artists are nothing if not persuasive; don't listen to the typical lines, "I was sent by your insurance company," or "I've done work already for your neighbor up the street."

Sometimes it's hard for honest folk to believe that anyone would be capable of swindling people in trouble, especially the elderly. Most people *are* honest; but we're not talking about honest men and women here. We're talking about lowlife salamanders.

And, just in case any lowlife salamanders are reading this,

please take warning: Don't even think of practicing your bunco wiles in San Antonio. In the words of Officer Perales, "We think they're sorry individuals that take advantage of our senior citizens. . . . And if we don't get 'em, God will!"

Let Me Paint Your Roof

Home-repair swindles are deliberate rip-offs by people who pretend to be legitimate tradesmen. Sometimes they go so far as to paint a company logo, like Ace Construction, or Acme Furnace Repair, on their pickup trucks. These are not incompetent or over-priced handymen; they're professional crooks!

Brown and Marie Winton were out in their yard planting a lilac bush when a maroon pickup truck with black trim pulled up. It was a beautiful October day in Landrum, South Carolina, and Marie wanted to finish up her gardening before the sun went down. At 70, she never knew when she might wake up and have her arthritis start bothering her again. Watching the two men and the young boy get out of the truck and approach the yard, she wondered what they could want and hoped they'd soon go on about their business. One of the men was about 60, the other 35 or 40. The boy appeared to be about twelve years old. All of them were dark, but Marie couldn't guess their nationality.

"They said they had finished a paint job in Inman and had some paint left over, and if we let them paint the roof for advertisement they would do it free," Mrs. Winton later told a reporter. "They said they would put a plaque in the front yard if we would just give them a good name. I told them I didn't want the roof painted, but they kept saying, 'let us try a little here, let us try a little there,' and before I knew it, they were up on the roof."

The three then began to paint, speaking with one another in a foreign dialect and addressing the Wintons as "mom" and "pop." The older man apparently liked to talk. He said he had not been educated because he was an Indian, and

Indians had not had schooling when he was a boy.

Not only was he an Indian, he went on, but he was a good Christian as well; that was why he did such fine work. A great many people would do shoddy work painting a roof, he knew, but he was not one of that kind. He wanted to make sure that people knew what good work he did. He also said, in case anyone was interested, that his mother was 104, and made medicine up in the mountains. This paint he was using had a tar base, and wouldn't come off with a hose, because it was boiled...

After a while the men came down from the roof and began to add up expenses for what they had said would be a free job.

"They claimed to have used thirty-two gallons of paint on our roof," said Marie Winton. "If they used three gallons, I'll drink it."

According to the calculations of the workmen, when the roof was finished the Wintons would owe them $750.

"Well, I'm a diabetic on insulin, and Brown takes heart medicine," Mrs. Winton said. She told the workmen that they couldn't afford it.

When the Wintons refused to pay, the two men became belligerent. Marie Winton went into the house to call the police and one of them followed her, positioning himself between her and the phone so that she couldn't dial. Finally, when she saw that her husband was shaking, Marie became afraid that he would have another heart attack—he had already had two—and urged him to give the men $500 so that they'd leave. The men stood over him as he wrote the check.

"I've been had!" Brown Winton said when they had gone.

It is unclear why the Wintons did not immediately put a hold on the check and call the sheriff's department at this point, especially as they knew that they had been swindled. Law-enforcement officers who deal with bunco cases say that elderly people are often too humiliated to report such incidents to police.

The Wintons did not call the sheriff's office until the next day, by which time the painters had cashed the check and disappeared from the area.

A sheriff's officer said that such flimflam artists generally "hit an area and move on quickly." He also said that the fraud was similar to those committed by "what we call Southern Gypsies that operate out of Aiken [South Carolina]. . . .They half-finish a job, get their money, and leave."

That day it rained, and the "tar-base paint" stained the chimney, washed off the roof, and spoiled the flowers in the garden below.

Swindlers Foiled

The mobile home park in Bradenton, Florida, is a quiet place to which to retire. You can boat and fish on the deep, brown river that runs past the park, and watch the many kinds of birds that live there. Alligators share the river with the other wildlife, but the retirees don't have much to fear from them. It's the con men who prey on Florida's elderly citizens that they have to watch out for.

Viola Cranston, a seventy-nine-year-old inhabitant of the park, poked her head out the window and saw that two men were painting her mobile home. She told them she didn't want any painting done, but they assured her it was free because of her age. She went back inside, feeling confused and frightened, and soon afterward the men knocked on her door and gave her a bill: $2,400.

Mrs. Cranston told them that she didn't have that kind of money at home, and the men told her that they would drive her to her bank, First Federal Savings and Loan in Cortez Plaza, so that she could take it out of her savings account. Fortunately for Viola Cranston, Betty Kelso, a vice president at the bank, was suspicious when she heard her elderly customer ask to withdraw the money, and she called the police.

When police arrived, they saw two men in a pickup truck driving back and forth in the parking lot outside the bank. They arrested the suspects, Robert D. Gag and Robert B.

Lee, and the two were charged with grand theft. Viola Cranston has identified the men as the painters who drove her to the bank.

The men have denied that they charged any more than $400 for the paint job. Police discovered a clipboard with the figure $2,400 in the pickup, but Lee allegedly claimed the figure was an estimate for work to be done on the truck. The two men have been released on bond awaiting trial.

Smooth-Talking Contractor

Homeowners in Westchester County, New York, have recently discovered that the contractor they describe as "smooth" and "slick" is slippery as well.

"This man could talk you into just about anything," said one of several known victims of the con artist, who may or may not also be a construction contractor. While he was great at bidding prices for repair and remodeling, the only job anyone has actually seen him perform is a snow job. One woman told the press that she had paid him $6,000 in advance, and another woman had paid him $9,000 so that he could buy materials to get started on a home remodel. After giving him the money, neither woman could ever get ahold of him.

Another homeowner wanted her kitchen remodeled. She overheard him talking with some people at her bank about home improvement and was so taken with his air of trustworthiness and self-confidence that she asked him to give her an estimate on her kitchen.

"He quoted me this unbelievably low price," she said.

In this case, the spurious contractor did come in with a work crew, but the result of their visit couldn't exactly be called home improvement. For $1,500 they took apart her kitchen, "ripping everything up." Assuring the woman that he had everything he needed to begin work the next day, the contractor left with his men—and that was the last she saw of him.

Another woman had a similar experience with the contractor; he took $1,500 from her and then "he and six men totally dismantled every room in my house. He promised me it would all be done in two weeks," she explained. After ripping up the house, he confided that he was a little low on cash for materials and payroll, and asked for another $4,500 in advance before he began building in the house. The housewife, who said later that she had felt a little sorry for him, paid.

Eventually, people who had given the contractor money up front began to get suspicious. They were able to get together and compare notes, since he had asked everyone he dealt with to refer him to others who needed work done. When they tried calling him at the number listed for his business on the printed receipts he had given them, they reached a delicatessen in Newburgh, New York.

Victims have filed complaints with the Westchester County District Attorney and the New Rochelle Police Department. Authorities are conducting an investigation, but have refused to say how many complaints they have received from dissatisfied customers, or to give a description or name of the contractor.

You Won't Take Me Alive

Bill Cochrain, a fifty-nine-year-old contractor who has been operating in Claiborne County, Tennessee, for fourteen years, has accrued at least twenty outstanding civil court judgments against him. None has been paid. Weeks after Cochrain had failed to appear in court on a criminal fraud charge, a bondsman and a sheriff's deputy visited his home to find him and bring him in. The latest charge against Cochrain was for allegedly swindling a woman out of $6,000 as a down payment for extensive work on her house which he never did. Cochrain is different from other swindlers in the home-repair line in that he doesn't get out of town while the getting's good, but prefers to lie low around home.

The contractor, who has a reputation for spinning tales to get jobs and then absconding with advance payments, did not appear to be home when the two arrived. The gate to the fence around his house was locked. The sheriff's patrol car had a loudspeaker which the deputy used to identify himself and to tell Cochrain to come to the door. No answer.

The deputy and the bondsman reported that the house was locked, too. They broke in and began to search for Cochrain, whom they found buried under a pile of quilts in the closet.

"He grabbed a coat hanger. . . and came out fighting and scratching," said the bondsman. "He just grabbed anything he could find. He bit my hand and I've got a big bruise on my arm, but there's no teeth marks. I think maybe he just gummed me."

Cochrain alleged that the bondsman had hit him over the nose with a crowbar. When told of Cochrain's accusation, the six-and-a-half-foot, 325-pound bondsman replied, "He said that?

"There was no crowbar. If anybody had been hit with a crowbar, it would've been a lot worse for him than it was."

Case of the Outworn Welcome

A seventy-four-year-old Salem, Virginia, woman, who prefers that her name be withheld, was held captive in her home and threatened by four people for about six months, Salem police said. For the first half of 1985, one of the four was allegedly always with her. They told her that two people living in the basement would kill her if she said anything, and that her phone was tapped, according to charges.

Police said that the four did some repair work and pruning around the house, for which they charged her several thousand dollars.

"They were doing jackleg work and receiving expert prices," said Salem Police detective Lieutenant Russ Gwaltney. He said that, although the woman had relatives in Roanoke County, she was too afraid to tell them what was happening to her.

Police did receive an anonymous tip that something was

amiss, however, and another elderly Salem woman was sent out to "maneuver the woman away from the suspects." When the police picked her up, the victimized woman broke down and blurted out the whole story, as if she had been under an unbearable strain.

John Ashton, 22, and his wife Shelly, 31, Ron Bixby, 30, and Nancy Quentin, 22, have all been charged with abducting the woman and obtaining money from her under false pretenses. Quentin has also been charged with grand larceny. Gwaltney said that about $275 in silver was stolen from the woman, but has been recovered.

The following stories involve old-time con techniques that have changed very little over the years. No matter how often these cons are used and how much publicity they receive, they never seem to go out of style; people continue to fall for them.

Pigeon Drop

Mansfield, Ohio, Police Lieutenant David Messmore recently got a chuckle out of a pigeon-drop scam that took place in a local shopping-center parking lot.

An elderly woman, who asked not to be identified, was approached by two well-dressed young women as she was about to get into her car. The women asked her whether she had dropped a wallet that they claimed to have found near her automobile. She told them that it was not hers. The two then explained that it was full of money, and showed her a thick wad of hundred-dollar bills. They had spoken to Mr. Weinstein, the owner of J.C. Penney's, they explained, and he had said that if the wallet did not belong to the owner of the car, then they could split the money—with the provision that each must put up some good faith money and turn the whole bundle in to him. Then, after a legally specified amount of time, he would divide up the cash and distribute it to them by check.

The young women offered to share their good fortune

with the elderly woman. She agreed, and the two accomplices drove her to her bank, where she withdrew $700, then brought her back to the parking lot. Placing her cash in an envelope with the supposedly found bills, they entrusted her with the whole amount, asking her to deliver it to Mr. Weinstein's office.

The elderly woman did as she was instructed, but no one at the Penney's store had ever heard of Mr. Weinstein. Sympathetic clerks, upon hearing her story, told her that she had been had, and contacted the police.

When the envelope was opened, however, it was found to contain $2,000! Apparently the con women had made a mistake when they attempted to switch the envelopes.

No arrests are anticipated, the good lieutenant said, because "It's not hardly a crime for someone to give you money.

"She could easily have been a victim," he continued. "I can't add too well, but it sounds to me like she just made $1,300."

It would have been entertaining to see the looks on the con women's faces when they opened their envelope and discovered that it contained play money or cut-up newspaper. Were they good sports about winding up on the receiving end of the con, I wonder, or did they gnash their teeth and dispute as to whose fault it was? We will never know. It is certain, however, that the elderly woman is thanking her stars that she came out of the incident ahead.

To Lieutenant Messmore, who has seen a number of such cases end less happily, the con artists' blunder was a stroke of serendipity.

"It's really heartening to see something like this happen. It's enjoyable," he said.

Can't Fool the Old Fooler

An alleged con woman was arrested in Denver, Colorado, in June 1985 due to what Denver police have termed "an Academy Award performance" by a seventy-seven-year-old woman who pretended to be senile.

The woman, whom police did not identify, was near East 10th Avenue and Grant Street when she was approached by a young woman who introduced herself as Carol Brown. Holding out a paper bag, Carol told the elderly woman that she had just found $196,000 in cash and $3.5 million in bonds. The sack also contained a note with something about gunrunning in El Salvador written on it, she said. After some conversation, she was able to convince the old lady to take her home so that she could telephone her boss and ask him what to do.

At the elderly woman's house, Carol made the call to her employer, who she said was an owner of a brokerage firm. He soon called back and told the women that it was all right for them to keep the money, but that they would have to open a joint savings account to cover any taxes that might be levied. He told the elderly woman to open an account with Carol and to deposit the $21,000 in it, and to also open a joint safe-deposit box for the money that had been found. Because this was a Saturday, she would have to wait until the following Monday to do the banking.

Carol Brown spent the weekend with the elderly woman, who later told police that she thought she was being swindled, but was afraid for her life. Finally she accused the young woman of trying to cheat her and started to call the police. Carol Brown ran out of the apartment.

The elderly woman did then call the police, and Detective Mike Fiori went over to her house in case the con artists decided to come back. Fiori told her that if she received a phone call from one of the suspects, she should say that she had been testing Carol Brown to find out whether she was trustworthy, and that she wanted her to come back.

Fiori was still there when the "boss" called, and the elderly woman followed the detective's instructions. Soon afterward Carol Brown returned; Fiori hid in an adjoining room to listen in on the ensuing conversation between the young con woman and her intended victim. The elderly woman pretended to be senile, and told the younger woman that she couldn't remember what she was supposed to do. After

Carol Brown had once again briefed her on all of the details of the scam, Fiori came out of his hiding place and arrested her.

"Carol Brown" is actually Julie Heil, a twenty-three-year-old resident of Grand Rapids, Michigan. She was jailed for investigation of theft over $10,000 and attempted theft from the elderly, and was held in lieu of $20,000 bond.

Bank Examiner Scheme

Sadie Majesky, 86, was spending a day much like any other at her home in Fresno, California, when the phone rang. Hoping it was her daughter in Minneapolis, she laid aside the afghan she was crocheting for her grandchildren and crossed the room to pick up the receiver.

It was not her daughter, but some stranger, a man who identified himself as Mr. Flores, manager of the Bank America branch in Calwa, where Mrs. Majesky kept her savings accounts. She was alarmed, thinking that she had perhaps made an error in her accounting. Since her husband died she had been having some difficulty in keeping her records straight. The time was when simple arithmetic had given her no problem at all, but these days even the most trivial details often escaped her, and she made mistakes. Getting old was no picnic.

"Oh, you've done everything perfectly correctly," Mr. Flores reassured her kindly. "We at Bank America have the utmost confidence in your integrity. That's why I've contacted you. Frankly, we have reason to believe that one of our employees has been embezzling money from our clients' accounts. This doesn't happen often, believe me, but every once in a while you get a rotten apple. I was hoping that you would help us to apprehend the thief—catch him in the act."

This was totally unexpected. Sadie liked to think of herself as a good citizen, but she felt suspicious.

"What do you want me to do?" she asked guardedly.

"Just transfer a portion of your savings to your time certificate account, and then withdraw the money after a day or two. I'll give you all of the instructions you need as you proceed and walk you through it. There's absolutely nothing to worry about," Mr. Flores said. His voice was authoritative and at the same time comforting. It was flattering to hear that the branch manager had confidence enough in her integrity that he would ask her to help him catch a crook, she thought. Still, something sounded a touch fishy.

"Well, I'm not sure," she told him. "I'd like to speak to someone else about this, if you don't mind, Mr. Flores."

No, he didn't mind, he understood perfectly, and in fact admired her for insisting that everything be completely aboveboard. He supplied her with a number to call as a reference; Sadie took her pencil and carefully wrote it down, then called the number.

"Fresno County District Attorney's office!" answered a businesslike woman's voice at the other end of the line. "May I help you?"

Sadie explained her reason for calling, and the woman confirmed all that Mr. Flores had said. "We would very much appreciate your assistance in this matter, Mrs. Majesky," she told the elderly lady.

Sadie's doubts were set aside, and she went to her bank and withdrew $3,500 in hundred-dollar bills and then took a cab to a local K-Mart parking lot, trying her best to follow the exact instructions of what she believed to be the district attorney's office. Waiting beside a parked car, a man greeted her, identifying himself as an investigator, and took her money. He then told her to go home and await a call from Mr. Flores.

The call came, and Mr. Flores was full of praise for Sadie's act, which he said was the mark of a good citizen. He was certain that they would be able to convict the felon, but they needed a little more evidence to wrap the case up. Would Mrs. Majesky please repeat the procedure, this time withdrawing $5,000?

A bank teller who had known Sadie for years was concerned about Sadie's sizable withdrawal. She cautioned her friend not to withdraw so much cash; surely it wasn't wise to carry fifty hundred-dollar bills in her purse! But by now Sadie was caught up in the excitement of apprehending a thief. She hadn't felt so involved in the life of the community for years, and had never been given the chance to perform an act of heroism until now. She wasn't going to let the moment pass; she might never have this opportunity again! She liked this bank teller, but probably the woman knew nothing of the operation; Mr. Flores had intimated that the employees at the bank were to be kept in the dark in order for the plan to work. Or maybe the teller *did* know and had reasons of her own for wanting to foil the plan. She had always seemed like a nice person, but Sadie had lived long enough to know that you never can tell about people. Maybe the teller herself was in on the swindle.

So, disregarding the warning, she once again took the money to the K-Mart parking lot and turned it over to the investigator. Then, overcome by the unaccustomed excitement, she went home to take a nap. A day passed, then two days. Sadie wanted to find out what had happened. Had they caught the thief? Had her mission been successful? Gradually her confidence began to ebb and, as the thrill subsided, a dreadful feeling of doubt began to assail her. She called the bank and asked for the manager.

The manager's name was not Mr. Flores. He told her he knew nothing of a plan to test the honesty of his employees. He called the police, and as of this writing Sadie is still waiting for the real criminals to be apprehended.

Variations on a Scheme

The following instances of the Jamaican hustle, also known as the handkerchief switch, all appeared in newspapers around the country during 1985, and show variations possible on a confidence game theme.

*   *   *

A Raleigh, North Carolina, man of 66 reported that he was conned out of a sum of money by two men whom he had just met that day. The first man appeared to be a foreigner, who approached the victim on Hargett Street in Raleigh, presumably to ask his advice. He wanted to invest his money, the foreigner said, but didn't trust American banks. He expressed the fear that, once he had made a deposit, he wouldn't be able to withdraw his funds. The victim then took the foreigner to his bank to show him that money could be withdrawn. To prove it, he took $2,300 out of his savings account.

At this point, another stranger, who appeared to be an American passerby who was also trying to help the foreigner, pulled a red handkerchief from his pocket and told the victim and the foreigner to place their money inside of it. Then he tied the ends in a knot and handed it to the Raleigh man, telling him to meet the foreigner the next day and help him to open an account at the bank, since it was then past five p.m. and the bank had closed.

Ten minutes after the strangers had left, the Raleigh man became curious and opened the cloth. Inside he found shredded newspaper. He reported that he was very embarrassed, as he was old enough to know better. The suspects were described as two black men, probably in their early thirties, one of whom pretended to be a foreigner.

*   *   *

A twenty-year-old man was flimflammed by a con artist who spoke with a Jamaican accent. He approached the victim in Orleans Square in Savannah, Georgia, saying that he was a stranger in town and needed a place to stay. The young man offered to drive him to a hotel. A woman then came up, and the Jamaican told her the same story. Soon, all three were driving off to the Ramada Inn on Oglethorpe Avenue. The Jamaican proposed a plan that would double the young man's money.

Following the Jamaican's instructions, he went to his bank and withdrew $500. The Jamaican then convinced him to put the money into a bag that supposedly held the Jamaican's money and told him to hold onto it while he ran a quick errand. He promised that he would soon return, and that the young man would then double his money.

The Jamaican, however, did not return, and, after several hours, the young man opened the bag and found newspaper scraps—but no money.

*   *   *

An Antioch, California, retiree was in K-Mart shopping for fishing equipment when he was approached by a middle-aged black man, over six feet tall and probably weighing about 250 pounds. When he smiled, the retiree noticed that several of his teeth were gold; when he spoke, it was in an accent the retiree had never heard. The man was certainly not American.

The black apologized for interrupting the other man's shopping, but said that he had a problem. He was from South Africa, he explained, visiting California in order to settle the estate of his brother, who had died in the Soviet shooting of KAL flight 007. He was trying to find a black charity in Pittsburg, and asked the fisherman for help.

"You want to be good to people," the retiree later said. "He needed help in a strange country."

Another man happened along, and the South African asked him for the address of the charity. The second man told him the place had burned down.

Then the South African politely asked the retiree for a ride to a house where he was staying. The second man decided to come along too. Soon the South African was telling another tale, and the trip to the house was forgotten.

It seemed that he had $150,000 in his pocket, the insurance settlement for his brother's death. He would be punished for bringing the money back into South Africa, he said, and added that he would burn the money if he could not find a suitable charity before he had to return to his native land.

"If you're just gonna burn it anyway," the second man said, "I sure could use $10,000. How about you?" he asked, turning to the retiree.

The retiree allowed he could use some extra money, seeing as how it was going to be burned up otherwise.

The South African agreed to give each of the men $10,000 if they would promise to each put $65,000 of his money into a worthy charity after he had gone back to South Africa.

In order to show that he could be trusted to find a charitable institution and was not accepting the responsibility simply because he wanted the money, the second man got out of the car near a bank and said that he was going to withdraw $2,500 from his account. The South African then asked the retiree if he would do the same.

The retiree, who by this time suspected he was being conned, got out of the car to hold the back seat up for the South African so that he could slide out of the vehicle. "I don't want any part of this," he said, gesturing for him to get out.

The retiree thought that his passenger might argue or threaten him, or refuse to leave the car until he got some money. To his surprise, the stranger said mildly, "you're a real nice man," and walked away.

*   *   *

In Pekin, Illinois, an elderly man was approached by another man, about 35, who said that he was new in town and couldn't find a certain hotel he was looking for. The old man said that there was no such hotel in town, but that he would drive him to a Holiday Inn.

As the car was maneuvering out of the Wendy's lot, the stranger saw another man walking up to the restaurant and asked the driver to stop and check with him if he knew where the hotel was. The second man got into the car and said that they would pay the old man $100 to take them both to the Holiday Inn.

On the way, the out-of-towner said that he needed a job. The second man told him his uncle was a manager at a Hardee's restaurant, and suggested he go there to apply for a job. The old man drove him to Hardee's. While they waited in the car, the second man drew out a deck of cards and told the old fellow that they could probably beat the new guy in town at cards, and get some of the money he had been flashing around. The elderly man agreed, and when the stranger came out of Hardee's, they all began to play cards in the Hardee's parking lot.

As the game progressed, the stranger, who was betting heavily, began to lose hand after hand. He refused to pay the other men their winnings, however.

"If I win," he said, "how do I know you can pay me?"

This made sense to the old man, so he went home, leaving his two new acquaintances out in the car while he asked his wife for the bankbook.

When his wife had heard what he wanted it for, she told him no dice.

"It sounds like a con to me," she said, "and you're not taking any money out of the bank for such foolishness."

Not one to be told his business by the little woman, especially when he had an audience of two other men, the old man went on over to his bank and wrote a counter check for $1,500.

After several hours the old man, who was way ahead, said that he had better be getting home. The stranger took his $1,500 and placed it in an envelope with his winnings, a wad of bills supposedly containing $2,300.

Before getting out of the car, the stranger showed him how to pull the envelope out of his shirt to amaze his wife when he got home.

"Always carry your money next to your heart, like this," he said, buttoning the envelope up in his shirt. Then he removed it again with a flourish—and laid it on the car seat next to the old man before getting out of the car.

When the old man pulled the envelope out of his shirt, his wife was not impressed. She wanted to look inside. When she opened the envelope, they saw it contained—you guessed it—shredded newspaper.

Bunco Shorts

The following are miscellaneous bunco schemes of the ordinary, everyday kind, all of which occurred during 1985.

The first three are examples of what is called "Gypsy crime," because they follow centuries-old Gypsy rip-off patterns, although Gypsies are not the only perpetrators of such scams. Gypsy crime is still practiced today, most especially on the West Coast.

*   *   *

An elderly woman in Monticello, New York, was approached by two women. One, calling herself Cindy, was about 30, with light-brown hair and a snaggle-toothed smile; the other, who used the name Margaret, was about 50, with an Eastern European accent, pale skin, and a heavy build. Margaret wore a pillbox hat and a brown trench coat, granny glasses, and big gold hoop earrings.

The two strangers told the old lady that Cindy felt ill, and asked if they could come over to her house to rest.

As the Monticello woman prepared them a pot of tea in the kitchen, one of the women ransacked her bedroom, stealing heirloom jewelry and other objects.

After the women had thanked their hostess and left, she discovered the theft, but didn't call police for two hours because she felt upset and embarrassed.

*   *   *

Another pair of con women—or perhaps the same pair—victimized a ninety-three-year-old Greenwich, Connecticut, woman in a similar way. First they helped the old lady across a street to her apartment and asked her for a glass of water. While the elderly woman was getting them their water, the two stole a large amount of her silverware.

*   *   *

In Forest Park, Illinois, an elderly couple was robbed of $400 that they were keeping in a teapot in their kitchen.

They were expecting a roof repair crew to arrive that day, so when three men showed up at their door claiming to be roofers, the man and woman let them in.

As soon as they were inside the house, the three men began to pester the couple with questions and requests in an apparent effort to distract them. One said he had to get some hot water from the basement, another asked for change for a twenty, while the third requested a glass of water.

While the couple ran here and there fetching things for the workmen, the three seemed to disappear. Suspicious, the man removed the teapot lid and looked inside, only to find that his money was gone.

All three offenders were described as being in their middle twenties, and are believed by police to be Gypsies. They were driving a black pickup truck with nothing in the bed area and no writing on it.

* * *

A clerk at the Comfort Inn in Valdosta, Georgia, was short-changed by a customer. First, he pumped five dollars' worth of gasoline into his van and paid the clerk with a twenty.

The clerk gave the man change: a ten and a five.

The customer told the clerk that he wanted to give back the five along with four ones in exchange for a ten. The clerk agreed and the man gave him one five and four one-dollar bills.

The man then took the ten and asked the clerk to count the money, and the clerk did so.

"Comes to nine dollars," he told the customer.

"Tell you what," said the man, "I'll give you a ten and a one for a twenty, and we'll call it even."

The clerk gave him a twenty, he handed over a ten and a one, and then drove away.

* * *

Two con artists stole an estimated $200 from Madray's Deli in Conshohocken, Pennsylvania.

Two well-dressed men in their late twenties entered the deli and began to look around. They did not appear to know each other.

The first man bought a pound of cheese. The second man then bought a can of beer and asked for a cigar. To get him the cigar, the clerk had to turn her back on the two men. Customer one, leaving his cheese on the counter, said, "Could you keep this a moment for me? I want to browse a bit more, and I don't want to carry it around."

Customer two asked the clerk for more cigars, and once again she turned her back, leaving the register open, and got down the cheroots from a high shelf behind the counter.

"Hey," the second man said, "that guy just left and forgot to take his cheese. I'll run catch him and tell him." Taking his cigar, he rushed out of the store.

A little later, the clerk noticed that ten twenty-dollar bills were missing from the cash register.

$$* \quad * \quad *$$

In Everett, Washington, a citizen lost several hundred dollars to a team who based their pitch on the pretense of promoting interracial trust. The scam started off like a Jamaican hustle; the victim was approached by a black man who claimed to be new in town and in search of a place to stay. The Holiday Inn was decided upon, and the victim offered to drive him there. While en route to the Inn, the black man placed a fifty-dollar bill in the ashtray as payment for the ride. At the Holiday Inn, the rider said, "This isn't the right hotel!" A passerby was asked whether he knew of another place to stay in the area. They all went out to the parking lot to talk it over.

As they chatted, the subject turned to race relations. The rider and the passerby, both of whom were black, said that they would prove they trusted the driver, even though he was white. They gave him some money in an envelope and told him to walk away with it, then come back. He did so. Then they said for him to put money in the envelope, and they would walk away with it.

After the white man had put his money in the envelope and handed it over, the two men began to walk slowly away. Gradually, their speed increased, until they were streaking across the parking lot. Soon they had totally disappeared into the dark, foggy night. The victim waited quite awhile, but they never came back.

As he drove away, he noticed that the fifty had also disappeared from the ashtray.

Plastic Crime

Bonnie and Clyde were born too soon. Today they wouldn't need guns; modern bank robbers make millions armed only with plastic. Credit card fraud, the fastest growing crime in the United States, has become a lucrative career for con artists, forgers, counterfeiters, and others who want the rewards of robbery without the concomitant danger of dodging bullets. While they live and work everywhere, they are most active in New York, Los Angeles, and South Florida, the three biggest plastic crime centers in the world.

The cardholder may pay up to $50 for every one of his credit cards or card account numbers used illegally, but it is the issuing banks that bear the brunt of credit card fraud. Visa's losses jumped from an estimated $740,000 in 1981 to $39.3 million in 1984. According to the Federal Trade Commission (FTC), annual combined losses to consumers and the credit card industry may now exceed $700,000,000. Losses are passed along to the consumer in the form of increased credit card rates and fees and higher prices for merchandise.

You may have been the victim of credit card fraud if you have ever received a Visa or MasterCard statement that billed you for purchases you never made—even if your card was still safe in your wallet. Using methods which will be described below, swindlers commonly rip off card holders using only their account numbers and expiration dates, as well as by actual card theft. In either case, you are not held liable by law for the unauthorized use of a card that you have already reported lost or stolen, and, in any event, your maximum liability for someone else's unauthorized use of your credit cards is $50 per card. (Only a letter—not a phone call—made within thirty days of the questioned billing will protect your rights under the Fair Credit Billing Act. The letter should contain your account number, the purchases in question, and your reasons for questioning the charges.) The procedure sounds straightforward enough, but you will be questioned and perhaps asked to swear that you did not make the purchases in question. The process takes a long time, and the hassle involved is daunting.

Credit card fraud takes many forms, from simple theft and subsequent use of hot cards to elaborate counterfeiting techniques. Sometimes an accomplished grifter in possession of a lost or stolen wallet will use the so-called Good Samaritan ploy: He calls the owner and says that he has found the wallet and will return it at a certain time. The owner, relieved, does not report his cards lost or stolen. This gives the crook time to run up a number of purchases, or to copy the account numbers and expiration dates for his own use. A variation on this ploy is used by a con artist who has both an automatic teller bank card and access to its owner's telephone number. Posing as a bank employee, he calls the owner and explains that someone has turned in the lost card, but that he will need the secret identification code in order to safeguard the owner's account in case the card was fraudulently used before it was returned.

Credit-card counterfeiting, rare before 1981, according to law-enforcement officials, cost Visa and MasterCard companies, combined, nearly $60 million in 1984, and the problem has continued to grow. There are four basic kinds of credit-card counterfeiting: manufacture of cards, using valid numbers and expiration dates; alteration of expired cards; use of bogus credit-card sales receipts in cooperation with a merchant; and telephone and mail-order fraud, in which only valid account numbers and expiration dates are necessary. (This fourth category is considered counterfeiting although no plastic is actually used.)

Counterfeiters who manufacture cards use sheets of white plastic cut to the correct size, or buy or steal blanks from manufacturers. The plastic is silkscreened with the desired logo, then imprinted with letters and numbers using an embossing machine, such as a Farrington. A Farrington machine may be bought from a large office-supply house for about $5,000. Department stores use embossing machines to make customer charge cards, and these are sometimes stolen or borrowed by store employees for counterfeiting purposes. Scratched, smeared or faded paint and uneven lettering are telltale signs of forgery to someone with a trained eye.

By altering the face of an existing card, genuine credit cards may be counterfeited. The plastic is heated in boiling water so that the embossed figures return to their original, flat position. Some counterfeiters use a hot iron for this purpose. Then, with an embossing machine, new letters and numbers are imprinted. Altered cards can often be recognized by small squares around letters or numbers, caused by pressing too hard during embossing, and by uneven lines at the borders of the logo, caused by heat distortion.

Counterfeiters in league with dishonest merchants supply valid names and expiration dates to forge cards which, though crude in appearance, work well enough to be put through a sales-charge machine. Charge slips are run off for bogus purchases and sent by the merchant to the bank. The merchant is paid by the bank long before the cardholder receives his billing, and the card issuer takes the loss.

The fourth type of counterfeiting, by far the most popular, does not involve forging or tampering with cards at all. The swindler simply places orders for merchandise by phone or mail using other people's account numbers and expiration dates.

How do counterfeiters get ahold of all those valid account numbers and expiration dates? Methods vary. It can be as simple as going through the trash, or as complicated as setting up a phony business. If your number was stolen, it could have happened in the store where you made a purchase.

Employees of stores and restaurants routinely throw away the carbons from credit-card charge slips, and scroungers can find a treasure trove of valuable information in the dumpsters outside such businesses. Sometimes, too, dishonest employees will keep carbons and sell them to grifters. Often driver's license numbers used as ID are written on the sales slips, and the impression of the number will come through on the carbon. Even if you write a check rather than use your card you may unwittingly give out your credit card number. You may have noticed that a merchant demands more identification to take a check than to accept your Visa or MasterCard, and the reason for this is simple. If he is stuck with a bad check, he, not the bank, must make good on it. So long as he follows the basic procedure for accepting a credit card—checking the number against a weekly list of stolen and cancelled cards, and, if the amount of purchase is over fifty dollars, calling for authorization—he will not be liable for nonpayment by the cardholder. This is why the sales clerk asks for your driver's license, two major credit cards, and check guarantee card when she takes your personal check and then duly inscribes a veritable credit history on the back. Anyone with access to the cash register or daily bank deposit can make a note of all of this information, as well as your name, address, phone number, and bank.

A person so disposed is then able to compile a little dossier on you, which he may sell to a kit maker. The kit maker is an accomplished forger and counterfeiter. He uses the information to make credit cards and phony ID to back them up. These are in turn sold to a card passer, who runs up each card to its credit limit. After that, the packet may be sold in turn to another passer, who carefully keeps purchases under the fifty-dollar limit so that sales clerks won't call in the cards for verification. Credit card slips and carbons from the trash of auto-rental establishments are useful to the kit maker, as they come complete with driver's license numbers and addresses of cardholders.

Credit-card counterfeiters sometimes go to great lengths to obtain large numbers of valid numbers and expiration dates. Employees of banks and credit institutions have been generously bribed to deliver microfiches, each containing the names and account information of as many as 10,000 people. Or a counterfeiter may open up a phony, or shell, business, obtain authorization from a bank to accept credit card charges, and then place ads in the paper for great bargains. His prices are lower than anyone else's on mail-order merchandise. When the orders come pouring in, he and his employees write up sales slips, take them to the bank, and await payment. By the time the customers begin to wonder where their TVs and stereos are, the swindlers are already operating under another name in a different state.

In another fraud involving a phony business, a swindler obtained credit information on 223,000 people from a legitimate Georgia credit company, and then used the information for credit-card fraud.

Steps are being taken to make counterfeiting more difficult. In 1984 credit-card fraud became a federal crime and penalties were made more severe. The Secret Service, a branch of the U.S. Treasury Department, also received authorization and funding to investigate credit-card forgery as part of its currency police work. Visa and MasterCard are using new technology, incorporating electronically embedded account numbers, carbons that do not transfer account numbers, and fine-line printing visible only under ultraviolet light. Visa has come up with a hologram card and a terminal that can read information on the magnetic strip on the back of the card and verify information on the front. MasterCard is working on an integrated circuit card with a tiny computer chip. The cardholder will need a secret number to gain access to the card. This so-called smart card will have a memory of 64K, enabling it to store transactions and information, and identify its owner. MasterCard may also use a three-dimensional emblem and a patch of rainbow colors produced by laser technology on its cards.

Does this mean that the glory days of credit-card counterfeiting are numbered? Not according to Florida's Fraud and Theft Information bureau, whose officials gloomily remind us that microchips can be purchased by crooks, and that computer information can be easily simulated or duplicated. According to many law-enforcement officials, organized crime is heavily involved in credit-card counterfeiting, which will continue to be easier and more profitable than counterfeiting money, especially for frauds entailing only name and numbers rather than plastic. With the money behind organized crime, new technology can also be copied. A machine used to apply holograms can be purchased for about $17,000, for example, and ultraviolet ink is readily available.

If credit-card fraud continues to increase, the consumer will pay for it in the form of higher rates and prices.

If new technology reduces credit-card fraud, the consumer will also pay for the technology in the form of higher rates and fees. Still, I'd rather pay more for a card than be ripped off by scammers like those in the following stories. It's the principle of the thing.

"You Have Our Personal Guarantee!"

Some time last summer, a friend of mine showed me a red, white, and blue brochure from a company with an official-sounding name, offering her either a Visa or a MasterCard for a one-time fee of twenty-five dollars. She was excited, but apprehensive. The truth was, she told me, her Visa card had been revoked because she had routinely gone over her credit limit; the temptation to overlook such restrictions when a treat was in plain view had always been her downfall when it came to monetary matters. A lunch here, a trip to San Francisco there—that's the way the money goes—you know how it is, she sighed. I did know. But get back to the brochure, I told her.

Well, she explained, it made it seem so easy to get a new card. The issuing company stated that applicants' credit histories would not be checked. The only stipulations were that a credit limit of $500 would be imposed for the first year, the applicant could not have a history of bankruptcy or credit-card fraud, and either a Visa or a MasterCard could be applied for, but not both. The company, she said, practically guaranteed her a card.

The brochure didn't look suspect; the language was low-key and the instructions were simple enough not to be misleading, but contained enough bureaucratise to be believable. I think my friend would have sent in the twenty-five dollars, but the brochure stated that applications had to be in by June 14, 1985, and she didn't get around to it in time.

Lucky for her. National Bancard Limited of North America (ANB), the company that issued the brochures, was a phony business set up for the sole purpose of raking in twenty-five-dollar checks and money orders. Orchestrated by William Claude Gaines, a thirty-nine-year-old Texan who also went by the name Nick Galeta, the scheme duped at least 4,000 people during a four-month period. On July 26, 1984, when Gaines was arrested, the checks were still coming in, according to U.S. Postal Service officials.

Gaines set up offices in New Orleans and Kenner, Louisiana, and in Shreveport, Texas, where employees opened mail and accepted toll-free calls for brochures. ANB advertised in newspapers and on television nationwide, except for Louisiana, where the operation was centered. By accepting only out-of-state customers, Gaines hoped to avoid prosecution for fraud by making it more difficult for authorities to locate him, according to prosecutors. New Orleans Postal Inspector James Mann said that at least 1,000 unpaid bills for advertising were found in ANB's offices after Gaines' arrest.

The scam was clever, well-organized, and sophisticated, appealing to a large market—those who would like to have credit cards, but whose credit histories prevented them from owning them. Perhaps, like my friend, Gaines should have quit while he was ahead. Acting on consumer complaints, the U.S. Attorney General's office and the Postal Service launched an investigation, and were able to arrest Gaines before he and ANB had time to vanish.

Gaines was convicted of eleven counts of mail fraud in October 1985. At this writing his sentence has not been set, but he faces a possible fifty-five-year prison term and fines up to $11,000 if maximum penalties are imposed.

When I found out that ANB had been a fraud, I told my friend about it, thinking that she would be glad she hadn't sent in the application after all.

"Aren't you relieved you were lucky enough to avoid getting taken in by that con?" I asked.

But she was blasé about the whole thing. "It wouldn't have mattered," she told me. "If I had sent it in before the cut-off date, my check would've bounced like a rubber ball. Listen, do you want to do lunch?"

Easy Come, Easy Go

Cuban-American con artist Arturo Hoyo (who has several other aliases), is smart enough to rake in a sizeable salary every year at a legitimate job. Smart enough, yes—but he probably wouldn't want to. It's so much more fun to outsmart hundreds of "stupid" marks, not to mention American Express and the *Wall Street Journal!*

Hoyo, now operating out of a half-way house to which he has been released after serving three years in prison of an eight-year term, has told media interviewers that he is reformed. He says that he wants to work as a crime consultant to help banks and credit-card companies protect themselves against con artists like himself. It is difficult to believe Hoyo, however, despite his charming manner and flashing smile. John Dorschner, a staff writer for the Miami Herald's *Tropic* magazine, discovered that the endorsements, news clips, and other references which Hoyo supplied to support his qualifications for a job as a topnotch crime consultant had been faked by Hoyo in a prison print shop. When Dorschner confronted him with his forgeries, Hoyo was not at a loss for words for long. He told the reporter that no one else could have made such daring and advantageous use of a prison print shop. The cons that Hoyo did pull off, however, are sufficiently impressive even without his embroidering on the truth.

Hoyo and four partners set up a shell business in Naples,

Florida, on May 30, 1982. They furnished a suite in a new office building with desks, typewriters, and WATS lines, named their fledgling phony company American National Electronics, and set to work to give it an appearance of respectability. In a con game, of course, appearances are everything.

Using his imagination and forgery skills, Hoyo received a membership in the Better Business Bureau of Naples and a BA-2 credit rating from Dun & Bradstreet. Meanwhile, one of his partners, a personable white-haired gentleman named John Egener, opened accounts at several banks under the name David Walsch. As president of ANE, he explained, he would be depositing large checks from American Express, but he would have to insist that the bank honor the checks without waiting the customary four days for them to clear. No problem, said bank officials, perusing ANE's apparently excellent credentials.

Hoyo struck a similar deal with American Express, convincing the company executives to send him money three days after he submitted sales slips, rather than waiting the usual thirty days.

On the basis of a letter of reference from a phony bank—another exercise in creative writing on the part of the con team—the *Wall Street Journal* ran a series of advertisements for ANE, giving the company a $50,000 line of credit. The ads featured amazing bargains on Pac Man software, the Sony Walkman and Walkman II, and Atari home game system. Customers were encouraged to place their orders by mail or by phone, using a toll-free number.

Hoyo and his confederates were deluged with orders for the nonexistent merchandise. For a little more than a week, they deposited checks from American Express and deposited personal and American Express checks. Using sales slips supplied by American Express, Hoyo wrote in real names and account numbers and added dollar amounts according to caprice. Hoyo charged varying amounts of money according to the ethnic origin of the last names of his customers, but all were for several hundred dollars apiece. The Naples Post Office complained that something was fishy; why should ANE receive more mail than the city government? Hoyo smiled and demurred, but when American Express officials announced that they were checking out the company, ANE suddenly disappeared. Investigators who visited the office found it empty; the crew hadn't left so much as a fingerprint behind. American Express lost $155,000, and the *Wall Street Journal* was out $38,000.

The con team split the money five ways, and Hoyo felt dissatisfied with his share, especially as the overhead they had paid for the office was so high. He dreamed up another business enterprise. This time he bought a rental-car company with an established account with American Express and a good reputation. He talked a salesman into lending him a Farrington machine for a weekend, and, using the names, account numbers, and expiration dates gleaned from his last venture, he ran off 1,000 credit cards.

On Monday, he returned the machine, saying regretfully that it would not be appropriate for his business. Once again he opened a bank account, asking that the customary holdover period be waived so that he could draw on funds as soon as they were deposited. The bank agreed. All he and his associates had to do was make out sales slips for hundreds of dollars each, send them to American Express, and wait for the money to roll in. Hoyo transferred funds from his business account to banks in Mexico, Venezuela, and Curacao. This time the team had taken American Express for $255,000 in a matter of two weeks. When they discovered that American Express was holding their latest check while it conducted an investigation, they cleaned out the office and split.

Hoyo probably would have gotten away with it, but Egener blew it. He tried to withdraw funds from an account in Hialeah, Florida, and was arrested. In an attempt to make a deal, he gave out the names of his associates. Hoyo was arrested.

While awaiting trial, for reasons unknown, perhaps even to Hoyo himself, he went to several banks and obtained loans in his own name, using forged documents to pose as a doctor or a wealthy businessman. In all, he borrowed $117,000.

Just Riding Around

On October 8, 1985, three Miami residents were indicted by a federal grand jury in Alexandria, Virginia, on charges of credit-card fraud. The following month all three were found guilty and sentenced to three years in prison and fines ranging from $100,000 to $200,000.

According to court testimony, Jorge Dijon, Gorge Gonzalez, and Lupe Hernandez were part of a major counterfeit credit-card ring based in Miami. The three rented a white Lincoln Continental in Miami and went on a week-long joyride, drawing more than $6,400 in cash from banks in Atlanta and Chamblee, Georgia; Chattanooga, Tennessee; and Washington, D.C. Once in Washington, they bought nearly $1,800 worth of merchandise. All of the advances and purchases were made possible by counterfeit credit cards; at the time of their arrest, the three were carrying 220 phony MasterCard and Visa cards as well as eight counterfeit New Jersey driver's licenses. The government alleged that the three would emboss legitimate numbers on cards which had been screened with a fake bank logo. The names were also fake, to correspond with the names on the false ID.

"What always gets me," said a police officer, "is that credit-card con artists go to a lot of trouble and put themselves at risk to make the cards and use them. But then all they want to do is drive around in big cars and throw money around and buy a lot of stuff they don't want. They don't seem to have any other goal than to look like big shots for as long as a scam lasts."

Fast Times in Weston, Connecticut

Three high-school boys in Weston, Connecticut, pulled off a credit-card fraud scheme that netted them more than

$7,000 worth of electronic equipment over a six-month period, according to police. For a short time, Rob, Sam, and Steve, 14, 15, and 16 years old, respectively, were the proud possessors of several Walkman radios and videocassette recorders, a ham radio, television set, miniature tape recorder, and computer parts and monitors.

Steve was considered by the other youths to be the brains of the operation. He didn't get good grades in school, but he had a photographic memory, which was useful for many activities he found more interesting than school. He had a part-time job in a bookstore, where one of his duties was to check customers' ID. He didn't find this much more interesting than school, except that it paid money. When he took customers' checks, he was required by his boss to ask for two credit cards and to write the account numbers and expiration dates on the backs. After he got off work, Steve noticed that the numbers would sometimes come unbidden into his head. He had no particular reason to remember them, but, once he had looked at them and written them down, they became part of the knowledge he stored in his memory bank. Far from considering this mneumonic quirk a blessing, Steve thought of it as a freak in his brain circuiting. Why retain such superfluous information?

Steve was bored by school and the bookstore, but he was not bored by computers. One Saturday, Rob showed him an advertisement for a home computer he wanted.

"I want to send off for it," Rob said, "but by the time I've got enough money saved it'll be obsolete."

"Not necessarily," Steve said slowly, studying the order form on the ad. There were little boxes for credit-card account numerals and expiration date numerals. Steve found a pen and filled them all in. Then he picked up the phone and called in an order on the toll-free number. When asked for an address, he paused only a second or two before giving the house number of the old McPherson place down the block. Nobody had lived there since Old Man McPherson died, a couple of months back. Steve had happened to glance at the number on the mailbox once when he was walking to school, and naturally it had stuck in his mind. And not only had it entered his memory bank, but he was able to access it immediately.

"Trick brain," he muttered.

"What did you say?" Rob asked.

"Oh nothing."

As the weeks passed and more and more merchandise was dropped off at the McPherson house, Steve developed a real appreciation for his gift. He had finally found something profitable that he was really good at. Sam and Rob, always amazed at Steve's memory, were now stupified with his success. On the days that deliveries were expected, one of them would go over to the McPherson place and tape a note on the door. "No one home," it read. "Please leave packages in garage. Thank you."

After dark the three young criminals would cruise over to the house in Steve's car and Rob and Sam would load the boxes into the trunk while Steve, at the wheel, acted as lookout. Some of the booty they kept, but to keep too much would arouse their parents' suspicions. They ended up selling most of it to schoolmates for pocket money.

Unbeknownst to the boys, Mrs. Dougherty, an elderly woman who had lived across the street from the McPherson place for thirty years, was keeping an eye on the unusual activities there. Why were all of these strange deliveries being made to an empty house? And what was in those boxes? Finally, as much from curiosity as from suspicion, she reported the matter to the police. At about the same time, Rob decided to call in an order for some expensive stereo equipment without Steve's help. The answering service employee who took the call thought he sounded awkward, guilty, and too young to be using a credit card. She too called police.

Police officers began to watch the McPherson place and eventually, with the aid of some further tips from Mrs. Dougherty, nabbed Rob and Sam as they entered the garage to pick up the goods. Steve drove casually away, and might have escaped arrest, had Sam not cracked under pressure and squealed on him, referring to the older boy as "the mastermind of the whole operation."

Sam and Rob were tried in juvenile court and released to the custody of their parents with a stern injunction to keep to the straight and narrow from that day on. Steve was tried in Norwalk Superior Court, and was ordered to follow a probationary program that, when completed, will clear his record.

Busted by the Delivery Man

Michael Carter had just turned 24 when he was laid off his job as a heavy-equipment operator. He had been earning good money in the excavation trade, but he hadn't put much away. The day he lost his job, he went on a drinking binge with three or four of his buddies; after he had sobered up, he wasn't sure how many buddies, beers, or bottles of Jack Daniels there had been, or where his meager savings had gone.

Lay-offs are a fact of life in the construction trades, but Carter took unemployment hard. He moved into his sister's house and began to collect compensation pay, but the check that came in the mail every two weeks or so wasn't enough for the basic necessities, much less the extras he wanted. One day, as he was thumbing through a mail-order catalog and wishing he could buy a set of weights, a thought came to him. If he had a credit card, he could have the weights just by filling in a few numbers. He didn't have a credit card—but that need not stop him. He could fill in someone else's numbers using a fake name, and have the goods delivered to his house anyway.

He mulled over the idea for a while, wondering how to get ahold of a credit card without actually stealing one. He considered petty theft beneath his dignity. A consumer tip on TV gave him his answer.

"And remember," the announcer was saying in a sincere voice, "always make sure to take your carbons when you make a purchase with your card. . . . A dishonest person can easily rip you off simply by using the information on the carbon."

Carter was accustomed to making dumpster runs at night, so his sister wouldn't have to pay for garbage pickup. She might start charging him rent, he figured, if he didn't help out a little around the house. That night, before he threw his trash into the dumpster behind the Mamba Restaurant, he climbed in and scrounged around in the debris. This wasn't pleasant, but with the aid of a flashlight he found what he was looking for—a handful of black, smudgy slips of paper. He was on his way!

He began to phone in orders for all kinds of merchandise to mail-order companies all over the country from his Norfolk, Virginia, apartment. He never had to leave the house; the things he wanted were delivered right to his door. And, since he used the toll-free numbers listed in the catalogs, it never cost him a cent. His initial nervousness about the scam gave way to pride, as he continued to benefit from the scheme without getting caught.

Carter ran his scam for about a year, until the August afternoon when he got busted—by a delivery man. He didn't suspect a thing when the four boxes from Wonderful World of Mail Order in Hollywood arrived. So excited was he to receive the adult videocassettes and the three 35mm cameras he had ordered, he didn't even look at the man who held out the receipt for him to sign. Carter took the ballpoint handed to him along with the receipt and wrote "Dallas Lewis" on the correct line. Then he lugged the boxes inside and closed the door.

Five minutes later Carter answered the doorbell again. There stood the deliveryman—and three uniformed police officers. The jig was up.

Police were tipped to Carter's activities, and Jack Latourette, an investigator with the check and forgery squad, was assigned to observe Carter. He had received information that a certain delivery company was to make a drop-off to Carter. In order to see whether the suspect would actually sign for the goods—and to catch him in the act if he did—Latourette contacted the company and asked for its cooperation. He was allowed to borrow a uniform and truck, and made the delivery himself. After Carter received the merchandise.Latourette was joined by the other police officers, and the arrest was made.

Michael Carter, who was described as acting "a little bit surprised when he found out who I was" by Latourette, has been charged with seven counts of credit-card fraud for the theft of $3,000 worth of merchandise, and at this writing is awaiting trial.

Counterfeiters Caught in Sting

Charles "Sonny" O'Day and his lifelong friend, Tony Dimitri, alias Anthony Deneuve, both twenty-five years old and both from New York City, were arrested in August 1985 at JFK International Airport. They had just boarded a jet for Fort Lauderdale but, as it happened, neither they nor their boyhood dream of becoming bigshots in Florida ever got off the ground.

As usual, it was Sonny who hatched their latest get-rich-quick scheme. He was working for minimum wage as a department store cashier, and every day he threw away hundreds of carbons from credit-card sales slips.

"One day it hit me," he told law-enforcement officers after his arrest. "Here I am cursing at these things for getting my hands all dirty when I crumple 'em up, and they could be making me a million bucks."

After work he took all of the slips out of the trash and carefully smoothed them out. He put them all into a paper bag, took them home, and called Tony. Together they copied the names and numbers from the carbons as they discussed and improved upon Sonny's idea.

The idea was this: The two would amass a huge list of valid names and numbers from credit-card sales slip carbons, which they would emboss on blank credit cards. Neither of them was much good at the finer points of counterfeiting—they had failed miserably two years earlier at forging driver's licenses—but that wouldn't be a problem. Card-sized plastic blanks with raised letters and numerals would work just fine, as long as the merchant who ran off the charge slips wasn't too particular. Sonny could borrow

the embossing machine and forge the cards at the department store after hours. Then they would locate a willing
merchant—one without too many scruples—to run off sales
slips for nonexistent purchases with the forged cards and
include them with his daily deposit at the bank. When the
payments came in, Sonny, Tony, and the storekeeper would
split the profits three ways.

The plan worked just fine; in fact, it worked better than
they had dreamed it could. Sonny found a place to buy
sheets of white plastic, which they cut up and embossed
with the names and numbers they found in the trash. Tony,
who worked as a bouncer at an expensive night club,
purloined carbons from the charge slips of high rollers,
customers whom he deemed likely to have high credit
limits. One merchant went in with them on the scheme, then
another. Word traveled quickly through the grapevine, and
soon Sonny and Tony and their counterfeit cards were solidly
in business.

At first they operated only with storekeepers they knew,
or with friends of friends. After a while they were getting
calls from complete strangers, and this made Sonny nervous. What if somebody ratted on them?

"Don't worry about it," Tony would always say. They
needed to keep contacting new accomplices because for one
merchant to turn in too many unauthorized numbers on
a regular basis would draw suspicion; the storekeepers didn't
want to take that kind of risk. Of course, he allowed, he and
Sonny were taking a risk by dealing with strangers, but, as
he put it, no guts, no glory.

On the other hand, Tony wished that, once new contacts
had been made, Sonny wouldn't open up so much. For
someone who worried about being ratted on, Sonny sure
did talk a lot.

For example, Danny Brewster, who ran the little wine
store, was referred to them by another shopkeeper with
whom they had done business. Danny seemed like a good
enough guy, but it made Tony nervous when Sonny told him
everything they were doing. He even bragged about their
upcoming trip to Fort Lauderdale, where they planned to

pull off a big heist with the help of employees and owners of eight stores. If everything went as well as they expected in Florida, Sonny told Danny, they would probably move there, or at least winter in the Keys.

Sonny and Tony boarded the jet and were already extinguishing their smoking materials and buckling their seat belts when they were arrested on charges of credit-card fraud by two FBI agents.

Seventy-one counterfeit cards were found in Sonny's carry-on luggage; Tony's back pocket yielded a list of ninety American Express, Visa, and MasterCard account numbers with corresponding names of cardholders.

Tony's intuitive distrust of Danny had been on target. The wine shop was a cover, and Danny was an FBI agent.

Tony and Sonny were indicted by a federal grand jury on charges of intent to defraud in connection with their plot with the eight Florida store owners. At this writing each man faces a $10,000 fine, or twice the value of the offense, or ten years in prison, or both.

Word has it that Sonny has tried to cheer Tony up with his "worst-case" scenarios. The worst thing that could happen, he says, is that they both go to prison. There they will "turn lemons into lemonade" as he puts it, by making all kinds of contacts and learning everything about computer programming. By the time they get out, maybe in a couple of years with good behavior, they'll be all set to go to work on another scam. Something bigger this time, something having to do with electronics. He hasn't formulated the plan yet, but he figures he can easily work it out. Someday, Sonny says, they are really going to make the big time.

Purse Snatch

In Wheeling, West Virginia, a pair of con artists operated a purse-stealing operation in the fall of 1985. As of this writing, the pair has not been caught. If they are like most petty grifters and con artists, they have probably long since moved on to practice their wiles in another state.

At 1:30 one Friday afternoon, Barbara Green received a phone call at work.

"Hello, D.P. Consulting, Barbara Green speaking."

"Ms. Green?" said the woman on the other end of the line. "I seem to have been delivered some mail that was meant for your office. Could you meet me in the lobby in five minutes, and I'll drop it off with you?"

Barbara Green thanked the woman and went to the lobby, but the woman was nowhere to be found. Walking back to her office, Ms. Green passed a man, about forty years old, slight and of medium height, with graying light-brown hair. She didn't think much about him until she discovered that her purse was missing from her desk. It contained a red wallet with thirty-five dollars in cash, a full box of blank checks, and a savings account passbook.

That same day, Teddi Tarr, of Northeastern Business College, received a similar call from a woman identifying herself as "Sandy." Ms. Tarr, however, was too busy to leave her work area, and told the caller to leave the mail at the front office. When no one came to drop off the mail, and when Ms. Tarr and several other witnesses saw a stranger lurking in the building, the police were called. By that time the stranger was gone. (He, in fact, matched the description of the con man who fleeced Ms. Green.)

Later that afternoon the dishonest duo struck again, this time with more success. Pam Evick, at Medical Park Professional Center, Tower II, received a phone call from a woman professing to be holding mail for her in another doctor's office in the building. The employees in that office told Ms. Evick that somebody was probably playing a joke on her. She didn't realize just how far the "joke" went until, at closing time, she searched for her purse and at last realized that it had been stolen. It contained $221 in cash, credit cards, a checkbook, and a check for $50.

Police conjecture that the man involved in the thefts had visited the business offices earlier in order to learn the names of the employees so that his partner could ask for them by name over the phone.

About a week and a half after the Wheeling purse snatching incidents, a rash of similar thefts broke out in Cincinnati, Ohio. Observers at three downtown locations described the suspects as a man in his mid thirties and a woman in her twenties, both redheads. A woman would call the receptionist at her place of work in a large office building to tell her that she has packages to be delivered. The caller asks the receptionist to meet her downstairs in the lobby. While the receptionist is away from her desk, an accomplice sneaks in and makes off with her purse. A short time later, the woman would receive another call, ostensibly from an executive at her card-issuing bank (but in actuality the purse thief), telling her that someone has just attempted to withdraw money using her credit card, but that the police have already notified the credit-card company that the card is stolen.

If the victim believes that the bank is already aware of the thefts, he or she will not bother to report checks and credit cards as stolen, and the thieves will have plenty of time to make good use of their purloined packet.

One woman who owns an art gallery in Cincinnati told police that the con artist seemed very pleasant and personable. He was wearing a pin-striped suit, gold watch, and red tie. He took a business card and the glass of wine she offered him. She didn't notice until later that he also took her wallet when he left.

Handbag and wallet theft, in which identification, credit cards, and checks are stolen as well as cash, provide the resourceful criminal with a ready-made kit, complete with identification. The loss of identification, checks, and credit cards is an inconvenience in the short run which can lead to greater inconvenience further down the road.

National Counterfeiting Ring

October 7, 1981, was an ordinary day for employees of Kimball Plastics Manufacturing Company in Montrose, California. Ordinary, that is, until a shift supervisor answered a knock at the door and suddenly found himself face-to-face with four masked gunmen. Forcing the employees to lie stomach-down on the floor of the plant, the robbers found what they were looking for: a cardboard box containing 6,835 blank BankAmerica Visa cards. The getaway was successful.

The gunmen belonged to a credit-card counterfeiting ring operating out of California, but perpetrating fraud in at least forty-two states. According to Denver detective Robert Thiede, Jr., ring members had access to a Visa computer. They picked people with legitimate accounts and exceptionally high credit limits, then embossed the blanks with the selected names and numbers.

Ring members apparently used the cards in order to live high on the hog. Charging airline tickets to various cities, they would stay in luxurious hotel rooms, dine at the finest restaurants, and then charge large cash advances in order to fly back to California.

Approximately 300 arrests have been made in connection with the counterfeit cards, and more than 4,000 of the phony cards were recovered by police. Hundreds of thousands of dollars in goods and cash advances were gleaned with the hot plastic before the scam had finally run its course.

"It really shook us up," said Sergeant Russ Meltzer, of the Los Angeles Police Department bunco and forgery division. "It has really made us aware of the magnitude of the problem with credit card fraud."

Boiler-Room Plastic Scams

"Congratulations!" says the solicitor on the other end of the telephone line. "You've won a trip to Hawaii, all expenses paid. Now, if you'll just give me your Visa account number and expiration date for tax purposes, we'll see that you get what's coming to you."

Sounds exciting—but before you get carried away, stop and think. Instead of winning a free trip, you may just get taken for a ride. Telemarketing fraud, nearly unknown before

1983, now accounts for 10 percent of all credit-card fraud. Here's how it works.

A multistate network of boiler rooms—offices equipped with banks of telephones and staffed with professional telephone solicitors, or yaks—is set up by a ringleader (known as the "operator"). The yaks select potential suckers to fast-talk from lists bought from credit-card companies or other businesses. Using any one of a number of pitches, a yak will try to extract credit-card numbers and expiration dates from the people who answer the phone. Shell businesses are established by boiler-room operators so that merchant's MasterCard and Visa accounts are opened at different banks. Names and valid numbers gleaned from "prize winners" are used on fraudulent sales slips for amounts usually ranging from $150 to $250. The phony charges are submitted to the target banks, and the banks pay the operators weeks before cardholders receive their monthly bills. Con artists used this system to defraud issuing banks of at least $20 million in 1984, and, despite media coverage of such scams, they are still being perpetrated across the country today.

One of the latest and best-publicized telemarketing scams, based in California, took the Cathay Bank of Los Angeles for $470,000; the Union Bank of Los Angeles for $407,000; First Los Angeles Bank for $315,000; and California First of San Diego for $234,000, according to a suit filed jointly by Visa International Services Inc., and Master-Card International Inc., in 1985. You may have received a call from the solicitors manning the phones for this particular scam. Two boiler-room operators have been charged with stealing more than $2 million from twelve banks between 1982 and 1984.

Religious and Spiritual Bunco

He who willingly gives you one finger will also give you the whole hand.

—Old Gypsy saying

The spiritual bunco artist, like any other bunco artist, profits by pretending to be what he is not. His pretense is greater than that of other swindlers, however, for he sets himself up as nothing less than the earthly representative of divine authority. This pose provides him with an all but foolproof cover. He can rip off the faithful with a smile while self-righteously referring any questions or accusations "upstairs."

"God works in mysterious ways," remarks the con artist smugly as he pockets his daily take and heads for home—or the airport, if things are starting to get hot.

He may have manufactured all of his own credentials—even the religion he preaches—or he may be a duly ordained bad apple in an established church. He may claim to carry on the tradition of Moses, Christ, or Buddha, and imply that to find fault with his acts is blasphemy. The fact that so many sincere and dedicated people have devoted their lives to teaching the holy scriptures he quotes so glibly makes his life all the easier, for he capitalizes on their good reputations and usurps the respect they have earned.

Gypsy fortune-tellers, generally women, trade on another ancient tradition: ripping off the gullible through so-called spiritual counseling. Gypsy fortune-tellers and other self-styled psychic advisors generate more complaints than any other kind of religious or spiritual charlatan.

Unlike the teachers of the great religions, the fortune-teller does not invite the seeker to bask in the clear light of spiritual understanding. Rather, the spiritual world she inhabits is as murky as an old goldfish bowl. She shares this lurid sphere with ghosts, demons, and other spirits, and will pass messages back and forth between them and her clients for a price.

A dishonest psychic adviser or counselor, or fortune-teller—and research indicates that there are many of these at work today—manipulates the people who ask for her help through their hopes and fears, particularly through their fears. Usually claiming to be doing "God's work," she pretends to help her clients by practicing prophecy, exorcism, magic tricks, and prayer. It is usually the desperate client who makes repeated appointments and not the one-time curiosity seeker who is ripped off. Crossing the Gypsy's palm with gold or silver is an old practice, and one which is still highly acceptable to fortune-tellers. Reports show that many now also accept credit cards—and keep them for personal use!

The First Amendment to the U.S. Constitution, in protecting our rights to freedom of religion and speech, also makes prosecution of religious and spiritual fraud very difficult. This is unavoidable, since none of us can presume to say what another man's religious beliefs should be. It is therefore only in very clearcut cases that one can hope to convict a practitioner of religious or spiritual fraud. The Bhagwan Shree Rajneesh's lawyers claimed that he was the victim of religious persecution, for example, even though he pleaded guilty to immigration fraud. Whether he has ever conned anyone in any other way, we must leave to the reader to decide for himself.

The following stories deal with people who have allegedly used religion as a cover for perpetrating frauds. Among them are the aforementioned Bhagwan; a pastor who swindled two old men who asked him to officiate at their funerals; a churchgoer who conned his minister and the

other members of the congregation, as well as the Social
Security Administration; a self-ordained minister-bookie
with a self-professed knack for prophecy; a voodoo-
practicing witch doctor; and a flea-market Gypsy exorcist.

Devil To Pay for Scheme

A diabolical swindle, in which Anglican clergy and
members of the landed gentry were conned out of at least
$313,000 in 1985, has been exposed in England. Derry
Knight, 46, a great hulk of a man who had previously spent
time in jail for various crimes, including fraud and rape, collected the money from people involved in the charismatic
movement within the established Anglican church. The
funds were donated to finance a battle with Satan himself,
led by Knight, who is, by his own admission, a victim of
occasional demonic possession.

The secret masters of Britain's Satanic orders, said Knight,
were prominent English politicians, including Viscount
Whitelaw, deputy Prime Minister. These powerful representatives of the Dark Forces led a 2,000-member cult called
the Sons of Lucifer, according to Knight. With the contributions he took in he proposed to buy magical "unholy relics"
in order to take over the cult and somehow free himself and
its members from bondage to the Devil.

Knight's personal struggle with Satan began at birth, he
claimed, when his grandmother dedicated him to Satan.
Somewhat later he underwent an operation in which two
metal disks were implanted in his forehead to somehow
ensure his fealty to the Evil One. At twenty, he became an
initiate in the Sons of Lucifer. Money was also needed, he
claimed, to buy himself a Rolls-Royce equipped with a
telephone; this was to avert suspicion on the part of Lord
Whitelaw and other alleged Satanic servants, and to allow
him to make phone calls to others involved in his cause (his
home phone, he said, was tapped).

Instrumental in advancing Knight's crusade was the
Reverend John Baker, parish priest of the village of Newick

in East Sussex. Mr. Baker earned a first-class degree from Oxford University, and has mastered eleven languages. He organized a donor's group to back Knight and brought such notables as Viscount Brentford, Viscount Hampden, and the Earl of March into the fray as backers of Knight's cause. He was also able to win the support of the Bishop of Lewes, Peter Ball, a monk who eschews the elaborate trappings of the traditional church. Ball does not wear church vestments and reportedly worships in a converted pigsty.

The Reverend John Baker was aware of Knight's criminal career, but believed that his many transgressions were proofs of his battle with Satan. After all, when you wrestle with the Devil, you're bound to lose a round or two. He believed that he had seen Knight fall into a trance characteristic of "demonic spirit infestation." Knight had been fighting to free himself from bondage to Satan ever since the age of twenty, when he met Christ on the roof of Hull Prison during a prison riot.

Knight's alleged religious scam had been operating for about a year when Bishop Eric Kemp of Chichester got wind of it and called for an investigation by a police fraud squad. Derry Knight was arrested and brought to trial; a jury convicted him on nineteen counts of fraud, after more than 100 witnesses had testified. According to testimony, Knight had spent much of the money he collected on high living and dissipation. Prostitution and fast cars were mentioned as two of the vices in which Knight indulged.

Knight countered the allegations by stating that he had squandered his own money on loose living, and had spent the donations on legitimate anti-Satanist efforts. He said that his business involved selling the services of young call girls who had received surgical operations to artificially restore their virginity so that they would appear to be "bona fide virgins" to customers.

Judge Neil Denison sentenced Knight to seven years in jail and ordered him to pay a fine of $72,500, calling him a con man and stating that he had cynically manipulated the Christian beliefs of many good people.

As for the good people to whom the judge referred, most

of them continue to believe that Knight's efforts were sincere. The Reverend Mr. Baker reportedly continues in his conviction that Knight was a Satanist fighting to free himself from evil, and not a swindler.

Fortune-Teller, Fortune Taker

In Los Banos, California, during the summer of 1985, Teresa Ruiz met a gypsy palm reader at a flea market. Mrs. Ruiz, an elderly woman who speaks little English, had been bothered by lameness in her legs and stomachaches for several years. A believer in palmistry and faith healing, she spoke briefly to the reader, who called herself Madame Rosa, with the help of a passerby who acted as translator. Madame Rosa told her that her physical ailments were the result of a curse, and that she could remove the curse for $220.

Mrs. Ruiz went home and called her granddaughter, Melissa, to ask if she would accompany her to Madame Rosa's as an interpretor. Melissa agreed, saying that, since nothing else had worked, the fortune-teller was worth a try.

The Gypsy instructed Mrs. Ruiz to get a new white handkerchief which she was to wrap around a tomato, an apple, and a orange. She was to "bless" herself with the wrapped fruits from head to toe, then remove them from the handkerchief and rub each over her navel for twenty minutes. This would remove the curse, Madame Rosa explained.

As Mrs. Ruiz's attempts with the fruits were not successful, she made a second appointment with Madame Rosa which was to take place at the palm reader's home. This meeting would have to be more private, the fortune-teller said; Melissa would have to wait outside in her car.

The Gypsy silently set to work to remove Mrs. Ruiz's curse by rubbing a tomato over the elderly woman's stomach. Then, puncturing the tomato with her long fingernails, she pulled out a slug. Indicating that she had been victorious, the Gypsy wrote down the figure "$12,000," and gestured in a meaningful way toward Mrs. Ruiz's purse.

Mrs. Ruiz, frightened, shook her head and protested in Spanish and broken English that she didn't have that much money. The Gypsy looked angry; she reached for the purse, opened it, and removed all the cash it contained, about $9,000. Melissa had been urging her grandmother to open a savings account for the money she had hidden in a family Bible in her bedroom. The $9,000 was Mrs. Ruiz's life savings, and the young woman was afraid it would be stolen. Reluctantly, Mrs. Ruiz had agreed, but had never got around to depositing the cash. It would have been safer stashed in the good book.

Feeling beaten, Mrs. Ruiz returned to the car, but was too ashamed to tell Melissa what had happened until about three weeks later. Melissa and other members of the Ruiz family contacted Madame Rosa in an attempt to get back the money, but the Gypsy was no soft touch. She claimed that Mrs. Ruiz had given her only $1,000 on her last visit, not $9,000. Not only was she going to keep it, she said, but she intended to collect the balance of what she was owed for her services: another $2,500!

The family called the police, who obtained a warrant for Madame Rosa's arrest. When officers arrived at her apartment, however, they discovered that she had moved out. Police say that, had Mrs. Ruiz willingly paid the money, there would be no case. If however, Madame Rosa had taken the money from the elderly woman's purse against her will, then she would be guilty of theft.

Witch Doctor

In September 1985, a twenty-three-year-old woman living in Lodi, California, went to visit a witch doctor. In the Mexican village where she had been brought up, belief in witch doctors is common. It is also more common in California than many people may think.

Police say that they have been aware of José Mendez Garcia for some time. He advertises his supernatural services and has business cards that bill him as a witch doctor. The young Lodi woman, who prefers to remain anonymous, had no doubt that Garcia was capable of exorcising evil spirits and lifting curses, according to police. She went to Garcia in hopes that he would change the run of bad luck she was having.

Instead, he threatened her with even more horrible curses. The young woman, who believed that she would die otherwise, was coerced into accompanying Garcia to Southern California. She took along her children, five-year-old twins, and they all stayed in a hotel room in Pacoima for nineteen days. Garcia made her have sex with him as a part of her treatment, using her superstitious beliefs against her, according to reports.

Her husband, back in Lodi, did not know what had happened to his wife and children or where they had gone until a man believed to be Garcia contacted his wife's relatives by phone and asked that money be sent to the hotel in Pacoima. When the woman's husband received this information, he drove to the motel where the witch doctor was holed up with his family and performed a citizen's arrest.

Police tried to convince the young woman to press charges against Garcia, but she repeatedly refused, as she was deathly afraid of his magic powers. She has since fled California and returned to Mexico with her husband and children. Without her testimony, law-enforcement officials say, they cannot hold Garcia or prosecute him.

One of the woman's relatives had told reporters that one of the twins was tatooed and poked with needles by Garcia during the kidnapping, but this was found to be untrue when the children received a medical examination. There was no indication that either of the children had been physically abused.

Seventh Time's a Charm

A thirty-five-year-old Tallahassee woman, whom we will call Frieda as she prefers that her name be withheld, was having problems with her husband and her employer. Having no one else she could really talk to, she often confided in an old friend who lived in Jacksonville, Florida. This Jacksonville woman swore by her fortune-teller and psychic counselor, a Gypsy who had many aliases, but who was best known as Madame Maria. She told Madame Maria all about Frieda's troubles, and asked the Gypsy to pray for her.

It didn't take Madame Maria long to get on the phone to Tallahassee. She called Frieda collect, saying that she had heard of her terrible situation and could help if Frieda wired her ninety dollars immediately. Frieda was filled to the brim with demons, declared Madame Maria, and the ninety dollars was a good first step toward exorcising them.

If some stranger calling herself Madame Maria called you collect and told you that you were full of demons, I doubt that you would continue the conversation. But Frieda was so distraught that she was willing to try anything. She wired the money and made an appointment to meet the Gypsy in a motel parking lot.

Frieda sat with Madame Maria in a parked car outside the motel and paid her $900. Then Madame Maria put a white handkerchief over Frieda's head and told her to close her eyes. When the cloth was removed and she was instructed to open her eyes, she saw a jar of water containing a tadpole on the car seat beside her. This apparent tadpole, explained the Gypsy, was in fact a demon which had been removed from Frieda's body while the handkerchief was over her head. While this may sound like a heavy rap to lay on an immature frog, Frieda apparently fell for it.

In all, she made seven payments totaling nearly $9,000 to Madame Maria in order to exorcise evil spirits or avert danger. In each case it was the Gypsy who made the contact, calling collect to warn the troubled woman about an impending disaster that could be avoided only by sending cash or valuables to Madame Maria.

Once the Gypsy told Frieda to send her all of her gold jewelry. She complied, mailing watches, chains, and rings worth more than $2,000. Another time she sent $800 in cash by parcel post.

When Madame Maria called collect for the seventh time,

something inside Frieda snapped. This time Madame Maria had overestimated her client's pliability. Frieda arranged a meeting in a motel parking lot as if nothing had changed, and then called the police.

Madame Maria's powers did not enable her to detect the change in her client's attitude, nor did she realize that the automobile in which they sat talking was electronically bugged. She was video-taped as she made her last demand for cash. Frieda handed her a final payment of $2,500, and the police moved in to arrest Madame Maria.

Trick or Treat

It was just before Halloween in 1985 that a Lancaster, Pennsylvania, woman was offered a chance to rid her body and house of evil spirits and demons. She had not been aware of any spirits and demons herself, but a house painter she hired informed her of their presence and offered her a once-in-a-lifetime deal: A friend of his, he said, would be able to perform an exorcism for just $8,000.

The woman played along with the ruse, but was not fooled. She called police, and a trap was set. The next day a young woman showed up as expected to perform the exorcism ceremony, which turned out to be surprisingly simple. Since she had been paid the $8,000, she said, the demons and spirits would leave the home. As she left the house, she was arrested by waiting police officers. The $8,000 used in the setup was play money.

Storefront "Church"

Sammy Fox, chief executive officer of a storefront "spiritual church" in Philadelphia, has recently disappeared. Police would like to know where he is, but for now Sammy isn't talking about his whereabouts.

Sammy's silence is uncharacteristic, for he is well-known as a man with the gift of gab. He has allegedly talked many people into believing that he also possesses the God-given ability to predict winning horses and lottery numbers. To further his scheme, police claim, he has used seven aliases to represent himself as a minister, soliciting new customers in several cities by mail. It is also alleged that he rented twelve post office boxes in different areas in order to receive incoming requests for guaranteed numbers, and that he used the storefront church in order to obtain a nonprofit mailing permit to keep postage costs down.

In 1985 a federal grand jury charged Fox with twelve counts of mail fraud. If caught and convicted on all charges, he faces a maximum sentence of sixty years in prison and a $12,000 fine.

Pastor Fleeced Strayed Sheep

Winfred Kahle, 75, and his brother Edward, 93, were not what you would call steady churchgoers. When they stopped to think about it, they realized that neither of them had been to church in forty-five years. The two got along pretty well on their isolated Minnesota farm, but as they were getting on in years, they decided that they should think about making funeral arrangements. They contacted the Reverend Frederick S. Cook, pastor of St. Peter's Lutheran Church in Moltke township.

The Reverend Cook allegedly told the brothers that he could officiate at their funerals, but only if they would donate $1,000 a year to the church for each of the forty-five years they had not attended services. The brothers agreed.

That agreement took place in February 1985. Eight months later the brothers had signed seven checks, all of which were allegedly made out by the pastor, totaling $30,000. The brothers were beginning to worry about their finances, and confided in a visiting nurse. She reported their story to the county sheriff, and an investigation was launched. During the course of the investigation, law-enforcement officials discovered that the $30,000 had been deposited in Cook's account, not that of St. Peter's.

Cook was charged with seven counts of theft by swindle

(one count for each check) and pleaded guilty to two counts totaling $16,200. At this writing Cook has not yet been sentenced, and the judge has not decided what disposition to make of the remaining five charges. Cook has resigned his post at St. Peter's, where he served as pastor for about four years.

The Miracle that Wasn't

There are accounts of religious leaders using their influence and authority to con others, but David Mott, a former hospital technician, conned his minister and the rest of the congregation of the Northside Christian Church in Claycomo, Missouri, as well as federal authorities, for four-and-a-half years.

In 1981, Mott, then 34, began to pretend that he had been stricken with multiple sclerosis and blindness. Church members pitched in to help, widening the door of his home to accommodate his wheelchair and raising money to help him pay expenses. Mott also accepted more than $40,000 in Social Security benefits.

Then one Sunday morning Mott stood up in church and confessed all.

"It's not a miracle that I'm standing here," he said.

If it wasn't a miracle, it was a shock to all, but the congregation and the Reverend Terry Rhoads said that they did not regret having helped him.

Mott, who called himself "a person who made a big mistake and owned up to it" in an interview with the *Kansas City Times,* said that he did not know why he had done it.

Wandering Bhagwan

After his November 1985 arrest at a Charlotte, North Carolina, airport, from which he and six close associates were allegedly attempting to flee to Bermuda, Bhagwan Shree Rajneesh pleaded guilty to immigration fraud charges and was deported. As he departed for India after the trial he declared bitterly, "I never want to return." Residents of the little town of Antelope, Oregon—renamed *Rajneesh* by the Bhagwan's followers—say the feeling is mutual.

According to federal charges, residents of Rajneeshpuram, the Rajneeshee commune in Oregon, committed immigration fraud under the direction of their fifty-three-year-old leader by participating in marriages of convenience with citizens of other countries. The Bhagwan was also charged with deliberately overstaying his visa on the pretext of ill health and of fleeing to evade arrest, but these charges were dropped on the basis of technicalities. Oregonians were angrier, however, about Rajneeshpuram's takeover of Antelope, a small town near the commune.

The takeover began in 1981, when the Bhagwan emigrated to Oregon from Poona, India, and set up Rajneeshpuram, a commune of people devoted to the Bhagwan's creed of Eastern mysticism mixed with popular psychology and eroticism. Years of warring with county and state governments followed, with threats of violence and considerable bad feeling on both sides. In 1984, thousands of street people from across the nation were persuaded by Rajneeshees to flock to the area in what was seen by Oregonians as an attempt to increase Rajneeshpuram's electoral strength. Commune members assisted the new arrivals in registering to vote and got them to the polls. The street people, who had been bused into Rajneeshpuram at Rajneeshee expense, for the most part proved ungrateful: Few of them were converted, and most left before the breakup of the commune.

Civil war broke out in Rajneeshpuram when the Bhagwan broke a three-year vow of meditative silence in 1985 to denounce Ma Anand Sheela, 35, his once-devoted disciple. He had placed Sheela in charge of the 3,000 members of the commune, as well as several thousand other *Sannyasins* (Bhagwan devotees) around the world.

"She had become addicted to becoming famous," Rajneesh said, "and this is a far worse drug than any in existence."

He also accused Sheela of such pranks as ordering her

"gang of fascists" to murder various people, including a street person, the Bhagwan's personal physician, and an Oregon district attorney; conspiring to poison the county's water supply; seeking to initiate an experimental AIDS treatment program which would bring AIDS victims into the commune and thus discourage strangers from visiting Rajneeshpuram; planning to divebomb county government buildings with one of his personal planes; engaging in electronic eavesdropping to maintain control within the commune; and embezzling communal funds.

"To Hell with Bhagwan," answered Sheela in an interview with *Stern* magazine in West Germany.

Having expeditiously hopped a plane to Switzerland the day after Rajneesh's arrest, she journeyed to West Germany, where a prosperous and comparatively diplomatic community of Sannyasins maintains eight Zorba the Buddha discos, as well as a chain of Rajneeshee restaurants.

Calling Rajneesh's allegations against her "total nonsense," Sheela told interviewers that she still loved him, but had left because she was tired of working for him like a slave. She expressed fear for her life, claiming that some Rajneeshees might try to kill her because she knew "everything about Bhagwan." She also accused her erstwhile master of studying Hitler's propaganda techniques in order to implement them himself. (Rajneesh, later watching a videotape of the interview, commented that she looked drugged.)

Shortly after speaking to *Stern*, Sheela was arrested for the murder of Rajneesh's personal physician. At the time of this book's publication, she remains in a Baden-Baden jail awaiting extradition to the United States, a process which may take months.

In December 1985, after the exodus of Sannyasins from Rajneeshpuram, an auction of abandoned belongings was held on the 64,000-acre ranch, and all monies taken in were applied to the payment of back taxes and other debts, estimated at $35,000,000. The commune contains an airstrip, a vinyard, restaurants, a shopping mall, and a Zorba the Buddha disco. On the door of the disco was taped a sign, which read: "Beloveds, the disco is closed from today on."

Robert Roethlisberger, the Texas car dealer who sold Rajneesh ninety-three Rolls Royces in various colors, comments publicly that he, for one, was going to miss the Bhagwan. To date, Roethlisberger has brought back at least eighty-four of the automobiles.

Before his extradition, the Bhagwan expressed a desire to resettle in his native India, but this would be difficult for him to do. During the Seventies, his ashram in Poona drew about 50,000 visitors a year. Then, in 1981, it was fire-bombed, and shortly afterward its tax-exempt status was revoked by the Indian government. The Bhagwan and a few associates hastily fled to the United States, leaving behind a host of surprised disciples and a huge debt, for which he is still held accountable.

So, scratch India. Rajneesh has so far been refused residence in Great Britain, Turkey and Greece. The Greek government has denied him refuge because of allegations that his followers have broken a national law against attempting to convert members of one religious faith to another. (There have been accusations that the Bhagwan, sometimes nicknamed "the swami of sex" in the U.S. press, has sought to institute free love as a religious practice on the Island of Crete.) The rumor is going around that Rajneesh may settle in Uruguay.

Back in the USA, the hamlet of Antelope is getting back to normal; and the U.S. Immigration and Naturalization Service, in part prompted by the Rajneeshee scandal, has instituted a new quiz as part of the procedure for applying for U.S. citizenship by marriage to a U.S. citizen. The quiz, intended to catch would-be immigration frauds, includes such questions as "What does your spouse take in his/her coffee?" and "What color is your bedroom ceiling?" The Service estimates that, of 111,653 applications for resident status by marriage in 1984, 30 percent turned out to be fraudulent. The number would be even higher if applicants were examined more closely, officials believe.

Black Hebrew Fraud

A twenty-month FBI investigation, involving court-ordered wiretaps and undercover operations, resulted in the indictment of thirty-two members of the Black Hebrew Israelite sect in September 1985. Five separate indictments were handed down by a federal grand jury in Washington, D.C., charging members of the religious group, also known as "the Nation," with financial fraud and conspiracy to racketeer for deliberately bouncing checks, engaging in credit-card fraud, defrauding telephone companies and their customers, transporting stolen property across state lines, forging airline tickets, and fraudulently obtaining welfare benefits from two Maryland counties.

During the course of the investigation, FBI agents discovered three Washington, D.C., locations that they allege were used as Black Hebrew safehouses for hiding fugitive sect members, as well as fake identification papers and stolen property. An "ID factory," in which members allegedly forged passports and driver's licenses, was also discovered on an old farmstead in Sheboygan County, Wisconsin. FBI spokesmen have said that they do not believe the sect itself to be a criminal enterprise, however.

The sect, which comprises an estimated two to three thousand members, was founded in Chicago by a former foundry worker. Its doctrine is based in part on the Old Testament, but also embraces polygamy and vegetarianism and rejects modern medicine. Members claim to be descended from the original tribes of Israel, and consider themselves Israeli citizens; the Supreme Court of Israel does not support this view, however.

During the Sixties, the Nation failed in its bid to settle in Liberia. Soon afterward, about one thousand Black Hebrews renounced their U.S. citizenship, and in 1985 Israel officially asked the United States to take them back. In the eyes of U.S. immigration authorities, however, these members of the Nation are no longer American citizens, and so they remain in Israel with no legal status.

Not easily discouraged, Black Hebrews persist in the belief that they are Israelis, and FBI officials say that the alleged criminal activities of sect members within the United States supplied overseas operations with goods and financial support. The federal grand jury that indicted group members has accused the Nation of using Biblical passages to "justify its criminal activities."

At this writing, the grand jury trial begun in 1985 is still in progress.

Charity Fraud

You can't cheat an honest man, or so the saying goes. Unfortunately for the honest souls among us, it isn't true. Con artists who engage in charity fraud disprove it every day by taking advantage of the compassion and generosity of men, women, and children around the country. Charity scams operate all year, but are especially prevalent at Christmastime and during and after large-scale catastrophes when the public desire to help others is particularly strong.

Charity swindlers work in three basic ways. They may take in money through the creation of a bogus charitable organization which may have either an original name, or a title worded to sound like the name of a well-known and respected charity; collect donations in the name of a legitimate charity without authorization, and then pocket the take; or raise funds under contract to a legitimate charity, and then split with the proceeds instead of delivering the contribution as promised.

Phony solicitors have fraudulently collected for such worthy causes as Meals on Wheels, the Red Cross, and local fire and police departments. Programs that benefit the handicapped, benefits for veterans, and, recently, AIDS research are also favorites of con artists. (A scam was recently discovered in Pennsylvania in which door-to-door salesmen collected money for magazines which were supposed to be sent to veterans' hospitals. Police believe that the money collected benefited only the operators of the scam, and that no actual magazines or veterans' hospitals were involved.)

Of all charities, those that help children are perhaps the

most universally embraced, and bunco schemes guised as fund-raisers for such charities have therefore been reliable money-makers for con artists over the years.

An old scam that takes advantage of children while purporting to help them is the door-to-door youth benefit scheme. Operators send young people out to canvas neighborhoods asking residents for donations to organizations with names that sound like those of legitimate youth-oriented nonprofit charities. Sometimes the child salesperson will give a little speech prepared by the operator stating that the sales program is keeping him off the streets and preventing him from getting into trouble, while at the same time teaching him the value of hard work. (Such speeches, apparently designed to appeal to the presumed prejudices of suburbanites, are usually delivered by black children in white neighborhoods.)

Donors may find the young salesperson difficult to refuse, and believe that they are helping to fund a worthwhile program. The operators of such scams, however, keep the money, paying the minors they employ very little. Furthermore, the products sold are generally of inferior quality.

This kind of rip-off is sometimes difficult to identify, since many legitimate, nonprofit organizations, including the public schools and the Girl Scouts, also send children out to sell wares door-to-door.

Give a Child Christmas, an organization in Saratoga Springs, Florida, that benefits needy children, was forced to quit soliciting door-to-door and outside stores in 1985. Why? Phony volunteers had been canvassing the area, taking contributions from people who believed that they were making the holidays happier for disadvantaged kids. In reality, donors were merely contributing to the well-being of a pack of scammers! In order to foil the imposters, Give a Child Christmas representatives issued a public statement warning Saratoga Springs residents not to contribute to door-to-door and shopping-mall solicitors who professed to represent the organization.

Also in 1985, at the height of the public hysteria over child abduction, one man collected at least $300,000 making telephone solicitations for donations to a non-existent locating service for missing children. Because parents had already been primed by sensational stories in the news media to fear for their children's lives, the swindler had only to cash in on the national paranoia. He displayed a typical con-artist trait—bare-faced audacity—when he called the Lost Child Network, a legitimate agency in Kansas, and asked for its endorsement.

"We said no way, and immediately gave his name to the federal authorities," said LCN President Craig Hill. The phony solicitor was later convicted on a mail-fraud charge in Kansas City, Missouri, for requesting donations for his nonexistent service.

Meanwhile, other scammers all over the country were out exploiting the widespread concern over kidnapped children. In Niceville, Florida, for example, a bogus publisher was selling advertising to local businesses for an upcoming magazine which was to be distributed locally, but which would supposedly contain photographs of all the children reported missing nationwide. A representative of the publication approached the Niceville-Valparaiso Chamber of Commerce several times requesting an endorsement. When the woman was told that the Chamber of Commerce was doing "some pretty heavy checking," she allegedly became nervous and disappeared. The self-styled publisher also disappeared at about the same time, leaving behind debts of $3,500 to advertisers as well as IOUs for back wages to several employees. The magazine was never published.

Child abuse, an age-old problem, caught the public's attention during the early Eighties, and naturally there were con artists ready to exploit the situation. In 1982 a woman established a foundation, ostensibly for the purpose of helping battered children, and began soliciting donations. The funds were to be spent on a ranch in Wyoming where abused children would be given a safe and happy second home. The woman took in more than $11,000 before authorities discovered that the plan was a ruse. In 1984 a warrant was issued for her arrest. Nearly a year later she turned herself in, and at this writing is out on bail, soon to undergo psychological testing to determine whether she is fit to undergo trial.

In some cases a charitable agency is legitimate, yet only a small percentage of donors' money goes to the cause for which it has been contributed. One reason for this problem is that professional fund-raising organizations hired by charities frequently charge exorbitant rates for their services.

Fund-raisers have also been known to make false claims while soliciting donations. Under a recently enacted state law regulating charitable solicitations, Oregon Attorney General Dave Frohnmayer filed charges against a fund-raising company for making false and misleading statements while representing two charities. In one case, the company sold coupon books for $14.95. Solicitors falsely claimed to be employees of the charitable organization, and led donors to believe that the entire amount would go to the charity; in reality, the fund-raisers kept $13.95 for every coupon book sold, according to allegations.

The same fund-raising organization is also charged with selling tickets to a country-Western concert under the pretext that the money would go to the National Fire and Burn Education Association. Ticket sales reached $12,000. According to a court petition for a restraining order against the fund-raisers, none of the proceeds went to National Fire and Burn, and Justice Department officials said no records existed on ticket buyers for the show. The concert was subsequently cancelled.

The state also seeks a court order that the fund-raisers refund all of the money they took in from concert ticket sales, and that they pay the charitable organization $7.50 for each coupon book sold in its name.

*   *   *

When you are approached for a charitable donation, take the following precautions to avoid being ripped off.
• Don't send money to organizations pitched by telephone solicitors using high-pressure tactics, or allow them to send someone over to pick up your check. Legitimate

nonprofit organizations seldom use such techniques to elicit funds.

- Find out all you can about a charity before donating to it. If you are asked for a contribution over the phone, ask for the name of the solicitor and the organization, as well as its address and phone number. Request literature to be sent to you by mail so that you can check it out for yourself.

- Don't be rushed into making a contribution. A legitimate organization has nothing to lose by allowing you to research its claims.

- Ask what percent of your contribution will go to administrative and general expenses and how much will go to the program you want to support.

- Check the name of the organization carefully for sound-alike titles designed to mislead contributors. The name of a bogus operation may closely resemble that of a reputable charity.

- Be especially cautious when purchasing household articles to benefit the blind or handicapped. Scammers frequently sell articles of inferior quality and give little or none of the proceeds to the causes they claim to represent.

- Don't feel you must make a donation because you receive a "gift" in the mail. Some companies will send such items unrequested to make you feel obligated to send money. According to federal law, you are under no obligation to return or pay for articles sent to you unless you asked for them.

- Find out whether the soliciting charity is registered with the Commission on Charitable Organizations, or a comparable branch of your state government. The Council of Better Business Bureaus also evaluates charities and reports on findings.

"Last Wish" Scams

Of all the charity shams practiced in recent years, none has incited greater indignation than those that falsely purported to grant dying children a last wish. There are several legitimate organizations that have carried out such programs over the last few years, and they have quite naturally appealed to the public. Donors have gladly contributed money for gifts that an ill child's parents, burdened with medical bills, cannot afford. Few people are left unmoved by the thought of a child who will not live to grow up; fewer still would seek to exploit such a child.

But there are exceptions!

*   *   *

An organization called A Wish With Wings (WWW) was established in 1982 in Arlington, Texas, to enhance the lives of chronically ill children. Such gifts as pets, trips to the seashore, and computers have been dispensed by the nonprofit organization. In 1985, employees at WWW began receiving calls from people who had been asked for contributions over the phone by anonymous solicitors. The contributions were to be sent to an address or picked up in person; the money was to go to "dying children."

WWW representatives said that the organization has never authorized telephone solicitations, and does not refer to the children it helps as "dying" or "terminally ill," but prefers to use the expression "children with life-threatening diseases." While it has become apparent that the name of the organization has been used fraudulently, at this writing the identities of the bogus solicitors are still unknown.

*   *   *

A Child's Wish Come True (CWCT), a charitable organization in Connecticut, has encountered similar problems. Its name was fraudulently used by a solicitor who collected donations from college students who believed their money would go to help a child who needed an organ transplant. The solicitor was caught and convicted of larceny. As it turned out, he had formerly been a legitimate fund-raiser for the organization, but had decided to free-lance in CWCT's name and keep the funds he collected.

*   *   *

The Genie Project, another charitable organization established to grant the wishes of terminally ill children, received a great deal of favorable press during the Eighties when its officers sent a child with leukemia to Disneyland. The Genie Project was shut down in 1985 when the State of Connecticut discovered that, of $237,000 taken in by the organization, only $10,000, or about four cents of every dollar donated, was actually used to fulfill the wishes of five children. The rest of the money, according to state charges brought against Michael and Suzanne Bates, founders and principal officers of Genie Project, was spent on payments to fund-raisers and salaries to three Genie officers, unsecured loans to project officers, $8,000 worth of jewelry purchased from Amway (the Bateses are Amway distributors), the rental of a videotape recorder and an X-rated movie called "Sex Games," and other personal expenses.

In the state's criminal case, which is still in progress, prosecutors have focused on the unsecured loans—about $14,000 worth—which the Bates couple allegedly reported to be secured by property they no longer owned. In the newspapers, the rental of the X-rated videotape paid with money from charitable contributions has often been given preeminence among the Bates' alleged crimes.

What with all the ado about the videotape, payments to professional fund-raisers by Genie have not been given much press. This issue may not be as titillating as a movie called "Sex Games," but it is certainly a more important one. Of $197,000 reportedly collected in the name of Genie Project by professional fund-raisers, only $42,000 went toward charitable purposes. The remaining $155,000 was retained by the fund-raising organization as its fee!

Disconcerting, Disappearing Defrauder

The Blind and Visually Impaired, a charitable organization based in Longview, Washington, was ripped off twice in 1985 by a fund-raising company. Frank Kenning, who also goes by the name Michel Kintzing, operator of American Promotions, has been charged with first degree theft by the Kitsap County prosecutor's office, but to date the suspect has successfully eluded lawmen. Authorities believe that Kenning has operated similar schemes in several Washington towns as well as in cities all along the West Coast. In a bulletin dispatched by law-enforcement officials, Kenning, 54, was described as being over six feet tall and weighing about 210 pounds, with gray, dark-streaked hair. Last seen driving a blue-green 1979 Cadillac and wearing a three-piece business suit, Kenning is fond of wearing "shiny jogging outfits," according to the bulletin.

Kenning was hired by the Blind and Visually Impaired to stage two concerts as benefits for the organization, one in Longview and the other in Port Orchard. Telephone solicitors hired by Kenning pitched the concert tickets as charitable contributions to benefit the blind; ticket-buyers could attend the gospel and jazz events themselves, or contribute them to handicapped children.

When Port Orchard ticket-holders arrived for the concert, they found that it had been canceled by Kenning without explanation. The Longview concert was held as planned, but, a charity spokesman alleged, the singer was never paid. Neither were the telephone solicitors, according to authorities, nor did the Blind and Visually Impaired receive any of the funds collected by American Promotions. The charity is apparently responsible for the telephone bill which the company's solicitors ran up, however.

When authorities discovered that Kenning had absconded with the proceeds from his fund-raising efforts, they confiscated accounting sheets from his operation indicating that he gleaned $10,306, $17,840, $18,000, and $9,220 from four separate charity fund-raising operations. All four are considered to be rip-off schemes.

Kenning did have excellent references from the Cowlitz County Sheriff's Office for a legitimate charity drive he conducted, however, and it was on the basis of this recommendation that he was hired by The Blind and Visually Impaired.

"That's how operations like this work," said Kitsap County Investigator Dick Kitchen. "They choose a legitimate organization and do a fund-raiser for them. They give them the proceeds and have a satisfied customer to use as a reference."

So if you're looking for a fund-raising company for a charity, and you find a guy who drives a 1979 Cadillac and wears a shiny jogging suit, don't hire him, no matter how good his references look.

All in the Family

An injunction to stop soliciting by telephone in the name of charity was issued against the Sterling family of Ardmore, Pennsylvania. The injunction was sought by the Pennsylvania attorney general, who charged that members of the family operated various fraudulent fund-raising enterprises, ostensibly to benefit charities, and deposited the proceeds in savings accounts under the name of Joshua Sterling.

Joshua, Naomi, and their daughter Maureen carried out their charitable scam through the White Cane Club in Broomal, Pennsylvania, according to the attorney general's office. White Cane telephone solicitors asked for contributions for nonprofit organizations including the Delaware County Association for the Blind and the Overbrook School for the Blind, as well as to fund White Cane purchases of Braille books and Seeing Eye dogs. In 1985 alone, the White Cane Club was estimated to have earned the Sterlings $140,000, none of which was forwarded to any agency for the blind. Agencies claimed by the Sterlings to be beneficiaries of the Club have publicly denied any connection with the Club.

While his parents and sister worked the club in Broomal, Joshua Sterling, Jr., was running another charity scam called the Palombaro Center, right around the corner. Using the telephone to request donations for handicapped children, Junior pocketed his take just as Dad was doing.

Or so the attorney general's consumer protection office believes, after receiving more than one hundred letters from contributors to Palombaro Center.

The attorney general's office has announced that if the Sterlings are found guilty, restitution will be requested in final orders. Victims of the scams may receive all or part of their money back. Legal proceedings are expected to take a year or more, however, and the court might order any money recovered to be turned over to a legitimate charity rather than to the donors.

Wheelchair Athletes

Padraic Cochran, a Colorado Springs resident, pleaded guilty to charitable fraud in October 1985. The twenty-two-year-old employee of Help, Ltd., a professional fund-raising organization, cheated forty victims out of about $10,000, according to court records.

Help, Ltd., was collecting money for a charitable organization called Colorado Wheelchair Sports Club when Cochran decided to moonlight by soliciting money for Wheelchair Athletes, a charity that didn't exist. One of Cochran's victims was an old man who was suffering severe dementia from Alzheimer's disease. Prosecutors said that Cochran repeatedly collected money from the man until his bank account was depleted. The elderly donor died before the case was brought to trial.

Marc Meyers, also known as Marc Montgomery , the head of Help, Ltd., was indicted in 1981 on charity fraud charges because he allegedly ran two telephone solicitation campaigns in which only 20 percent of the funds taken in were turned over to the charities for which they were raised. The charitable fraud statute was found unconstitutionally vague by the Supreme Court, and so the case against Meyers was dismissed.

According to the terms of a plea agreement, Cochran received probation in exchange for a guilty plea and was ordered to repay the donors he defrauded with 12 percent interest, cease to engage in charitable fund-raising work, and terminate his employment with Herbalife, a multi-level marketing company.

Earthquake Scam

After a catastrophic earthquake hit Mexico in September 1985, the American Red Cross accepted donations for a relief effort in that country. Meanwhile, donations were also being accepted by con artists posing as Red Cross representatives across the country.

Charges of theft were levied against a Cleveland man for soliciting donations under the pretense that he was the official representative in Ohio for the Red Cross Mexican Earthquake fund. A suspicious citizen called the police. When the man was asked for identification, the name of his supervisor, and the correct phone number for the Red Cross, police stated, he was unable to supply any of them.

Mexican-Americans in California were victimized by phony Red Cross solicitors for earthquake relief. Residents of Chico, California, reported solicitors who went door-to-door to request contributions. The Red Cross stated that no legitimate representatives of that organization were soliciting funds door-to-door.

San Francisco District Attorney Arlo Smith stated, "It is an unfortunate fact of life that whenever there is a worthy charitable cause, there are dishonest people who would take advantage of the human instinct to help those who are less fortunate. . . . Whenever there is a serious crisis where public financial support is solicited, the District Attorney's Office takes particular care to see that . . . the public is not being misled by charity swindlers."

The Riding Center

Julie Nelson was proud of her telephone solicitation job. For one thing, it was the first real job she had ever had. More important, though, it was worthwhile. She asked people to donate money to a riding center which had been set up for the purpose of teaching disabled children to ride horseback. It made Julie happy to imagine the kids having some fun and getting healthier and becoming more self-confident, all because of those riding lessons. According to Mr. Scamehorn, her boss, the program was really doing wonders. And she was a part of it!

One Saturday morning when Julie and the five other highschool girls who worked for Mr. Scamehorn showed up at the office, they thought maybe the place had been burglarized. The room had been ransacked, with file drawers left open and papers everywhere. Mr. Scamehorn didn't come in that day. After a while the girls went home and waited for him to call.

Mr. Scamehorn never did contact his employees again, but the police did. It was a shock to Julie to find out that her kindly employer had been operating a phony charity and that he had left town without paying her for all those Saturdays and afternoons after school that she had come in to solicit donations. The police knew that the girls had all believed that the riding center was a real charity. No charges were brought against any of them, because they, like the people who had made donations, had been tricked by Scamehorn.

Still, every time Julie thought about her job and Mr. Scamehorn, she felt sick at heart, even though she hadn't been aware of her role in the scam.

Jack Scamehorn, 40, was far away by that time, and had no plans to return to Livermore, California, any time soon. On three years' probation for writing more than $2,400 worth of bad checks in 1982 in connection with a prior business, he had a history of convictions for bad check writing and forgery dating back to 1971. When he established the riding center in 1983, he was forbidden by court order to have a checking account. Although he was not authorized to write checks on the riding center's account, he managed to do so anyway.

According to police investigators, only one child ever rode a horse at the center, and only once, after repeated requests by his parents. At least 650 people sent checks to Scamehorn's enterprise; there were also cash donations made to the center, although no records were kept of them.

Allegedly more than $17,000 of the charitable donations were spent on Scamehorn's personal business, as cancelled checks and other documents indicate. He would withdraw money for such things as birthday presents, albums, concert tickets, a correspondence course to become a private detective, vitamins, magazine subscriptions, a Hawaiian vacation, car repair bills, and bowling league dues.

When the charity scheme folded in 1984, Jack Scamehorn left town. Soon afterward he was charged in municipal court with two felonies, grand theft and forgery; a warrant is out for his arrest. Scamehorn was sighted in Arizona once, but at this writing is still evading arrest.

Insurance Fraud

Even to rank amateurs in the rip-off business, insurance companies are considered fair game. Padding claims for property loss is common practice for many otherwise honest people, who wouldn't dream of stealing from anyone else. The claims adjustor will probably find something in the small print to invalidate half of what he claims, anyway, the policy holder figures; he has to cheat a little just to stay even.

If all insurance swindlers were like this policy holder, thousands of insurance investigators would be out of a job, and our health and auto coverage would be a lot cheaper. The fact is, however, that there are insurance fraud professionals out there who earn all or a substantial part of their living by making out on false insurance claims. Who pays for the industry's losses? Everyone who takes out an insurance policy.

Automobile insurance scams provide a livelihood for many cheaters, from auto-body shop owners to organized crime figures. The auto fraud ring, say Insurance Crime Prevention Institute (ICPI) officials, is a postwar phenomenon. Born during the affluent period following World War II, automobile insurance fraud became a major crime industry during the Seventies, and the problem has not decreased in recent years. Faked car accidents and thefts are the bread and butter of ring members, who profit by collecting on property and casualty insurance claims. The insurance industry divides faked auto accidents into four categories: caused, intended, staged, and paper.

The *caused* accident is a sort of demolition derby, in

107

which schemers riding around in an old jalopy seek out well-insured victims with whom to collide. The victim vehicle is likely to be a bus, taxicab, or expensive, late-model car. A favorite accident-causing ploy of such demo crews, especially on the West Coast, is the *swoop-and-squat* maneuver. It involves two "bad-guy" cars and one "good-guy" car. Bad guy number one positions himself in front of the good guy in moving traffic. Bad guy number two then swoops in front of bad guy number one and brakes suddenly (in auto insurance lingo, he *squats*). Bad guy number one then brakes, causing the good guy to back-end him. In any caused accident, several passengers ride along in the bad-guy cars so that they can all claim medical injuries, typically whiplash and loss of wages due to the accident. Medical bills may be faked, and sometimes doctors conspire with the defrauders to submit phony bills to insurance companies.

The *intended* accident is one in which two or more cars are involved in a planned collision; all of the participants are defrauders. Rental vehicles are usually used in this scam.

In the *staged* accident, there is no collision. Defrauders prepare a stage set, complete with banged-up junkers, broken glass, and other props. They then take photographs as evidence to submit to insurance companies and call the police, who write up an accident report. Such ploys are often discovered by insurance investigators because the same cars are frequently used in several different scams. Sometimes adjusters recognize a photograph which has been submitted as proof of damage to a vehicle in several different accident claims.

The *paper* accident is a forgery scheme which sometimes involves no actual vehicles. Paper cars are created in states where insurance coverage and registration can be obtained without visual inspection of a vehicle. Police reports are forged, obtained over the counter, or gotten through a police officer who is also a conspirator in the fraud ring. Appraisal reports, photos, and repair estimates and bills are all finagled or made from scratch by forgers.

An ongoing police investigation in Sacramento, California, involves a paper accident ring whose leader is suspected of initiating rings in six states, ripping off at least $4 million from insurance companies. By billing himself as a male mid-wife, the ringleader was able to get his hands on blank birth certificates by the gross. With blank Social Security cards and fake photo IDs, along with the faked birth certificates, ring members opened bank accounts, got plastic under various pseudonyms, obtained driver's licenses, and then registered and insured cars provided by the mastermind leader. These were all late-model automobiles bought cheap, since they were totaled at the time of sale. Accidents were dreamed up for the vehicles by the leader, who had a lively imagination. He would brief his followers on invented accident details so that they could submit claims to their insurance companies. One insurance company reportedly paid for the same damaged Trans Am five times.

Professionals working in phony-theft rings commonly have participating car owners park their vehicles in designated spots, leaving them unlocked and with the keys in the ignition. Ring members drive them away to "chop shops," where the vehicles are dismantled. Motor-vehicle numbers are destroyed or altered, and the parts are sold through various fences. Meanwhile, the owners report their cars stolen, and collect on the insurance.

Another profitable variation on this theme is the staged auto accident. Photographs are taken, and sometimes auto-body shop owners or employees take part in the scheme, writing up lengthy estimates of damages to the vehicles. When the insured party collects on his claims, he splits his profits with the other conspirators.

The insurance industry has also had problems after floods and other natural disasters, when automobiles have been washed away or otherwise ruined or misplaced by acts of God. In the hubbub occasioned by such calamities, over-worked adjusters don't always have time to carefully check on each claim, and professional swindlers can cash in on policies, reporting vehicles as lost when they are actually sitting high and dry and unharmed in their driveways. While such cheating has been discovered on the part of amateurs, the industry also reports cases in which organized crime has been responsible for large-scale calamity fraud.

Ambulance chasing, more properly known as soliciting for a lawyer after an automobile accident, is another illegal but lucrative means of ripping off insurance companies. In a typical incident, which took place in Miami, Florida, in 1985, an insurance adjuster approached both drivers at the scene of a collision and told them, "If the insurance company needs any information, I've taken pictures." He then handed each of the drivers his card, which bore the same address as that of the lawyer he recommended. (The ambulance chaser need not be an insurance adjuster, but can be anyone acting on the part of a lawyer in order to drum up legal business as a result of an accident.)

Doctors and lawyers have also been known to conspire with one another in order to profit from clients' insurance claims. Ambulance chasers, or runners, may learn of accident victims by using police band radios or by visiting hospital emergency rooms. They then fix up the injured party with the lawyer-doctor team, which inflates his insurance claims, ensuring that he will collect as much as possible from the company. Some unscrupulous legal and medical professionals derive an excellent living from such practices. A typical case of a doctor-lawyer conspiracy occurred in Broken Arrow, Oklahoma, in 1985. A lawyer specializing in accident claims referred his clients to a local chiropractor. One accident victim visited the chiropractor four times, but was billed for eighty visits. The chiropractor submitted the inflated bill to an insurance company, but was investigated when adjusters recognized that the lawyer and chiropractor had often served the same client in reported claims in the past. The lawyer and doctor were charged with mail fraud, as is usual in such cases.

Faked accidents, known in the insurance business as "slip and fall" claims, are another means of defrauding insurance companies. Medical bills may be falsified, or are for difficult-to-diagnose ailments like headaches, nausea, and sleeplessness. There are even a few "accident victims" who purposely hurt themselves in order to collect insurance money!

Of all the insurance rip-off professions, there is none so dramatic as that of the "torch"—the man who burns down buildings for hire. He may work in a ring or as an independent, and is hired by property-owners who want to collect on their insurance policies.

When business is bad, small business owners may make more money by burning up their inventory than by trying to make a go of it. Businessmen facing bankruptcy may prefer to collect on insurance claims for their goods than to give it up to creditors. There are always more cases of small-business arson during times of economic recession for these reasons. Arson is suspected when account books and records are left out at the time of a fire, rather than locked away in fireproof safes, since the businessman is suspected of attempting to destroy evidence that he submitted inflated claims to his insurance company.

The insurance industry estimates that it loses more than half a billion dollars each year to arson. In most types of coverage, proof that the claimant caused the loss is enough to invalidate his claim. Fire coverage is different in that it usually indemnifies both the insured and the person who holds the mortgage on the property. Even if it is proved that the insured deliberately set the fire or hired a torch to do so, the company is still obligated to pay the mortgagee.

In 1971 the insurance industry established an independent investigative agency, the Insurance Crime Prevention Institute (ICPI) to check out insurance claims suspected of being fraudulent. This agency collects evidence of fraud from the file claims of different insurance carriers and uses the information to put together cases that can be tried in criminal court. Claims adjusters who suspect fraud call in the ICPI to check out the claimant. A claim that exhibits more than two or three of the "indicators" listed in Appendix A is likely to be suspect, according to ICPI guidelines.

So much for the plight of the insurance companies. We do not want to give the impression that the insured is the sole perpetrator of insurance fraud; this is a game that can work both ways.

In a recent case, unfortunately not unusual, internal

investigators at Prudential Insurance Company of America tipped off New York State police when they found that one of their salesmen was suspected of fraud. Apparently he had talked an elderly woman into giving him money so that she could collect a $65,000 payment on her late husband's life insurance policy. The salesman, who allegedly knew that the policy was still valid under a grace period, told the woman that it had expired. He offered to use his influence to make sure that she would receive the $65,000 payment in exchange for $20,000 she was eligible to receive from another policy. The salesman has been charged with felony grand larceny.

Insurance companies have also been known to use deceptive sales practices to trick customers into buying coverage they neither want nor need. In a case in Miami, Florida, the president of an Okeechobee insurance company has been charged with sixteen counts of theft and one count of scheming to defraud. Prosecutors say that customers who wanted only minimum coverage so that they could legally drive their cars have routinely been hurried and misled by salesmen into buying death and dismemberment policies as well.

One elderly woman was surprised to learn that she had bought a death benefit worth $5,000—that is, if she died after carrying the policy for at least three years.

"I just wanted to be able to drive my car," she testified.

Company lawyers countered that sales techniques used by the company were legal and that they "aren't that much different from those of other insurance companies."

In California, con artists have attempted to take advantage of auto accident liability insurance requirements by leafleting cars in Hispanic neighborhoods with advertisements for cheap, legal insurance. The leaflets, printed in Spanish, ask for payments of $250 to insure one vehicle, sight unseen, for a year, and another $50 for each additional vehicle. Payments are to be sent to a mail drop; the name of the insurance company is not listed with the insurance board, and the phone number given is a nonworking number.

Pickle Juice Conspirators

The pickle juice conspirators were a forty-nine-year-old housewife named Tiajuana Jones and her twenty-eight-year-old son, John, both from Oklahoma City, Oklahoma. The two allegedly motored off to McCartney's Food Market as if to perform a routine shopping trip. According to charges, however, once inside the store they proceeded to willfully and feloniously pour pickle juice on the floor.

That was only the beginning. While his mother looked on, John made a big show of sliding in the dill-scented liquid, subsequently losing his balance and crashing unceremoniously to the linoleum.

The two then lodged a formal complaint in order to collect damages. While the information provided by an issue of *ICPI Report* (October/December 1985) is admittedly rather sketchy, one can easily fill in the details of the scene that must have ensued. Picture Tiajuana, the distraught mother, villifying poor McCartney for indirectly causing injury to her boy!

If such an act was actually staged, it did not daunt ICPI investigators, who, during the course of routine procedures, uncovered the alleged fact that young John had been previously engaged in a brawl and had incurred his injuries as a result of the fight, not the negligence of store employees.

Tiajuana and John Jones were charged with one count each of conspiracy and making a false insurance claim. The outcome of the trial was not given in the *Report.*

Tooth-Devouring Onions

Within a period of one month, Dawn Simons, a resident of North Carolina, had the misfortune of breaking an upper front tooth three times while devouring a cheeseburger with onions. She blamed the onions on all three occasions, according to an article which appeared in the *ICPI Report.*

Insurers of MacDonald's and Burger King paid Simons $250 and $441, respectively; a steak house insurer, however, in surly fashion refused to pay.

Investigators obviously had two clues to go on, either one of which might reasonably have tipped them off that fraud was involved. First, how could Simons have broken the same tooth in the same way three different times? And second, given Simons' suspicions as to the cause of her alleged injury, why didn't she simply say "hold the onions" after the first mishap?

Simons was charged with one count of obtaining money by false pretense and insurance fraud, a misdemeanor felony, to which she entered a plea of guilty. She was given a suspended two-year sentence and five years' probation, fined $500, and ordered to make restitution of $441. She also had to pay her lawyer's fees and court costs.

That kind of money could have bought Simons a lot of cheeseburgers, and one hopes that she will take that fact into consideration the next time she thinks of claiming dental damage from onion mastication. It would have been cheaper, in the long run, just to get the tooth capped and forget the insurance claims. Another conclusion that might be drawn from this story is that, in the burger war currently raging among the fast-food establishments in the United States, Burger King has clearly scored a point for awarding the largest damage payment to a customer for onion-related tooth breakage!

Freak Auto Accident

A couple in Grand Rapids, Michigan, collected $9,000 in insurance benefits after what was at first termed a freak auto accident, according to the *ICPI Report.*

Joni Perks, 37, then insured, said that her car unexpectedly popped out of gear and lurched forward, breaking the ankle of her boyfriend, Peter Maus, 45.

According to investigators, Pete actually broke the bone when he fell down a flight of stairs that "climaxed a domestic dispute." Apparently he had no health coverage, or perhaps he had discovered the words "pays 80 percent of broken-bone costs, except when injury sustained during climax of domestic dispute" in small print in the back of his benefit summary booklet! The *Report* did not shed any light on this aspect of the story.

In any event, Pete was charged with one count of false pretense, and Joni was charged with one count of conspiracy to commit false pretense.

Do you think Joni could actually have *pushed* Pete down the stairs? If I ever find out how it turned out, I'll let you know.

Arson for Profit

Frank G. Elroy, the leader of an arson ring based in Pennsylvania, was convicted by a grand jury of four counts of arson in October 1984 and sentenced in 1985 to four consecutive two-to-four-year terms, one for each count. The arson-for-profit chief was also sentenced to a concurrent three-to-six-year term for failure to appear, as he fled to Florida to avoid trial.

Three members of the ring had already pleaded guilty: a torch, who confessed to setting three fires for Elroy; Elroy's brother-in-law, who allowed his truck to be burned under Elroy's supervision so that he could collect insurance money; and a former tenant of a rental building owned by Elroy. According to charges, Elroy had the building burned and the tenant filed a fraudulent insurance claim as part of an agreement with her landlord.

The man who was convicted of setting the fires was asked by the judge why he had performed such work for Elroy— couldn't he have found a safer, more honest way to make a living?

"It pays good," the torch replied. He was subsequently sentenced to one to five years in jail.

Elroy's brother-in-law was sentenced to ten years' probation and ordered to make restitution; the tenant was admitted to a rehabilitation program.

Store Torch

In September 1981, Donald Rubottom's Wichita, Kansas, auto supply store burned to the ground. Four years later, he and his wife, Dorothy, sued Hartford Insurance Co. for refusing to pay on his claim.

Representatives of the insurance company said in court that Hartford had not paid because "the fire at the Seneca Auto Supply. . .was intentionally set by Donald Rubottom, or he had it set."

"I don't know who set the fire, " Rubottom countered. "If I did, I would have had them arrested." He said that Hartford's case was strictly circumstantial.

What is the circumstantial evidence? Investigators said that they found thirteen gasoline-filled plastic jugs at the auto-supply store after the fire was quenched. Sheets of computer paper had been spread from jug to jug, they claimed, so that the fire would spread. Hartford also brought up Rubottom's shaky financial state as evidence that he was responsible for the fire; he had allegedly owed more than $53,000 in back payroll taxes when his business went up in flames. Furthermore, Hartford lawyers contended, he had increased his insurance coverage from $300,000 to $500,000 two months before the fire.

Rubottom said that the increase in coverage was necessary to insure his increasing inventory, and referred to his past history as evidence that he was not involved in insurance fraud. In twenty years of operating an auto-parts company, he had never before filed an insurance claim.

The federal court jury ruled that Rubottom had been responsible for setting the fire, and that Hartford was therefore not required to pay on his claim. Rubottom says that he can't afford to appeal.

Scheming Boyhood Buddies

Two couples were indicted in U.S. District Court in Philadelphia for running a ring whose purpose was to defraud insurance companies. The scheme, which ran from 1975 to 1985, bilked twenty-two insurance companies out of more than $1 million, according to charges.

Ralph and Sheela Higgler and Bill and Sarah Cassidy allegedly established fake ID, obtained credit cards under pseudonyms, forged signatures, and lied to police and in court documents in order to carry out various schemes over the ten-year period. According to court records, postal investigators studied documents for more than three years in order to compile evidence on the Higglers and Cassidys. Assistant U.S. attorneys said that the couples had faked boating and automobile accidents, slips and falls, baggage-claim losses, and automobile break-ins to fraudulently collect on insurance claims, and that ring members had also committed welfare fraud.

Welfare-fraud indictments charge that Sheela Higgler, along with other ring members, submitted false applications to the Department of Public Welfare for food stamps and other forms of public assistance; they allegedly lied about their marital status, and concealed ownership of savings accounts, real estate, automobiles, and a boat.

Ralph Higgler and Bill Cassidy, both Delaware Valley residents, were childhood friends: Sheela Higgler's father and sister, brother, and sister-in-law have also been indicted for participating in the ring. Authorities do not believe that the scam is strictly a family affair, however, and the grand jury is continuing to investigate doctors and lawyers who may have been involved.

The Higglers and Cassidys have pleaded not guilty, and all have been released on their own recognizance awaiting trial.

Justice Served

This shark attack hoax was just one of his schemes to get some money. I hope people don't hold me responsible.
—Harold Justice, Jeffrey's stepfather

If he flew right, he could have been a millionaire.
—Mike Kinster, Jeffrey's lifelong friend

*If somebody told me two weeks ago he'd steal my car, I'd
say they were crazy. . . . I don't really care what happens
to him anymore.*
—Cindy Heen, Jeffrey's former sweetheart

Seventeen-year-old Jeffrey Justice, extradited from Los
Angeles, California, to Fort Pierce, Florida, flew unescorted
back to his old stomping grounds on October 1, 1985. Upon
his arrival at Palm Beach International Airport, he was met
by several armed sheriff's deputies, who quickly ushered
him into a waiting car, to be delivered to the St. Lucie County
Juvenile Detention Center. The past month had been a hec-
tic one for Justice, but the bleach-blond youth, clad in blue
jeans, sneakers, a white T-shirt, and handcuffs, had a big
smile for reporters anyway.

The shark hoax planned and executed by Jeffrey Justice,
with a little help from his friends, Mike Kinster and Cindy
Heen, is the most bizarre insurance scam attempted in recent years—maybe the most bizarre ever. Justice, acknowl-
edged math genius and high school dropout, wasn't able
to pull it off, but he made a good try.

On September 5, 1985, Justice and Kinster rented a
fishing boat from the Taylor Creek Marina in Fort Pierce.
While at sea, the two discussed their plans for the day, which
were highly unusual. When they got back to shore, Kinster
was to tell the Coast Guard that Justice fell off the boat and
was subsequently eaten by a huge shark. Two $1,000 life-
insurance policies had been taken out by Justice the week
before, naming Cindy Heen as the beneficiary. While
everyone thought he was dead, Justice would secretly contact Heen and get the money, which he would share with
Kinster.

Mike Kinster had grown up with Jeffrey Justice in West
Virginia, and was accustomed to going along with his ideas.
He thought of Justice as "super smart," someone who "had

it all." Besides, Kinster wanted to pay off his car, and thought that Justice's scheme would be a good means to this end.

When they docked, Kinster rushed to report his friend's untimely demise, which he said occurred two miles out to sea and about four miles off Fort Pierce Inlet. Meanwhile, Cindy Heen picked up Justice at a public boat ramp near the South Bridge and sped off to Orlando with him in her red 1984 Pontiac Trans Am.

Cindy Heen loved this car above all else; it had been a present from her parents on her sixteenth birthday. As they traveled, Justice told Cindy about the hoax, leaving out the part about the insurance. As Cindy knew, he was on probation for forging two $3,000 checks, and he said that he was trying to avoid making restitution. Besides that, he wanted to get away from his mother.

The next day, under heavy questioning by St. Lucie County Sheriff's investigators, Kinster broke down and told all. The Coast Guard's exhaustive ocean search was called off, and a new search was begun for the young fugitive. Kinster didn't go anywhere for the next week, which he spent in jail. Afterward he was released on his own recognizance, charged with felony grand theft conspiracy for attempting to defraud an insurance company.

The news of the hoax quickly spread, and Justice told Heen that he was going to turn himself in to the authorities. Instead, he hung around Orlando and sneaked back to Heen's mobile home while she was attending freshman classes at the University of Central Florida. There he allegedly stole a Texaco credit card and jewelry estimated to be worth $4,500, including an antique ring which had belonged to Heen's grandmother. Then he took off in his friend's beloved red Trans Am. (Heen had expected him to pick her up after classes, but he, of course, never showed up. She reported her car as stolen September 13.)

Cindy Heen's mother came to stay with her after that, just in case the young man dared to show his face again. When asked by police for an explanation of Justice's behavior, the young woman reportedly replied, "He acts on impulse. He doesn't live a planned, balanced life. . . . He's one of those people who always had a lot of ideas."

Justice's stepfather, a truck driver, didn't think much of Jeffrey's ideas, which he said were just attempts to get money. "He always had the attitude of a rich kid; had to have excess money to keep up the appearance," he told reporters. He also said that once, when he tried to "discipline" his stepson, young Justice had called police to complain about child abuse.

Lieutenant Robert Provost, chief detective for the St. Lucie Sheriff's Office, however, reportedly said that part of Jeffrey's reason for attempting the insurance hoax was his conflict with his parents.

"He wanted to be independent and away from them. . . . He could be in China right now," a Florida newspaper quoted Provost as saying.

Justice's goals were more limited than that, though; his destination was California. On September 23, Los Angeles Sheriff's deputies saw Justice weaving along the Pacific Highway outside Los Angeles. They stopped him for crossing the centerline. When they ran a check on the Trans Am's license plate number, they found that it was listed as stolen. Officers also allegedly found a small rock of cocaine in the car, and Justice was arrested.

A public defender, who hoped to influence authorities to try Justice as a juvenile rather than as an adult, appeared to sympathize with the youth, who she said was afraid of going to prison. She also described him as homesick for Florida. As it turned out, the State of California dropped drug-possession charges against Justice so that he could be speedily extradited as a minor to Indian River County, Florida, where he was on probation. He will be tried as an adult, however on three felony charges in St. Lucie County—one count of conspriacy to commit grand theft in the insurance scheme, and two counts of writing worthless checks.

Justice's $200 check to the marina where he rented the boat bounced, as did a $50 check to Travelers Insurance Co., a premium payment for one of the life-insurance policies. The car-theft charge in Orange County, Florida, is still pending. Roger Heen, Cindy's father, said that the Trans Am is registered in his name, and that he will press charges.

And so we leave Jeffrey, Mike, and Cindy. Assistant State Attorney Thomas J. Walsh, Jr., said that Justice will probably not do much jail time—perhaps less than three months—because of overcrowding and because he has no prior adult record, even though he could receive a fifteen-year sentence if found guilty on all three St. Lucie counts. Cindy Heen hopes to get her car back, but her insurance company would rather replace it than pay for having it returned from California.

Mike says that he is not mad at his old friend anymore, although he was angry after the hoax first became public. The felony charge against Kinster has been reduced to a misdemeanor, because there is no proof that he knew that the insurance policies were for more than $100. He says that he wouldn't "stick around" Justice anymore, but admits that he was at fault, too.

"I feel like I did something stupid," he declared to a staff writer for the Stuart, Florida, *News*.

Cindy Heen says she isn't mad either, but doesn't want to see Justice again.

"It's so weird," she has been quoted as saying. "How can you care so much about someone and then have them do this to you?... He knew how much I loved that car."

Fleecing the Faithful, Texas Style

Clergymen and other employees of churches in twenty-seven states—including members of Jerry Falwell's Moral Majority, Inc.—have been swindled by Robert Redding in two separate but nearly identical scams, according to a Texas State insurance commissioner.

In 1980, Redding was sued by the Texas Insurance Board for failing to pay more than $300,000 in insurance benefits. Of these unpaid claims, $20,000 to $30,000 were due employees of more than 350 churches in the United Methodists' Central Texas Conference. An insurance board investigation had found that the Minister's Benefit Trust was bankrupt. According to Austin court records, the company was put in receivership in June 1983, but a number of the claims remained unsettled. Redding was put under a court order prohibiting him from engaging in any further insurance dealings in Texas, but Redding didn't let this little unpleasantness become an inconvenience to him.

He formed another Christian health-insurance company without filing for an insurance license, and so insurance investigators had no knowledge that he had violated the court order until policy holders began to complain. The second company, Christian Organizations Medical Society, has allegedly bilked $3 million from religious organizations in twenty-seven states and their foreign missions.

In 1985, after the Texas State Insurance Board once again brought suit against him for fraud, Redding filed for reorganization under Chapter 11 of the Federal Bankruptcy Act. The Texas Attorney General's Office says that he is hiding behind bankruptcy law in order to thwart a state investigation into his business operations. The state further contends that if Redding is allowed to reorganize under federal bankruptcy law, he will destroy records and continue to divert funds for his personal use; state officials recommend that Christian Organizations Medical Society be put in a state receivership or a federal trusteeship to prevent further "fraud, dishonesty, incompetence, and gross mismanagement."

Meanwhile, Redding's past and present policy holders are hopping mad. The wife of a Fort Worth assistant pastor said that she and her husband paid $2,000 out of pocket after the birth of their son when they were unable to collect from Minister's Benefit Trust.

"We had to pay it," she said. "But what made me really mad was to learn that he was still ripping off churches."

Holdup at the Main Office

In October 1985, Barry Kontax, charged by a grand jury

in Sumner County, Tennessee, with grand larceny, turned himself in, admitting that he fraudulently sold three insurance policies for which he pocketed clients' premiums. He has since been accused by five more Tennesseans, who say that he sold them insurance coverage they never received.

In one of the cases, according to law-enforcement officials, Kontax sold a policy for medical insurance to Fred and Bette Dougherty, a Portland, Tennessee, couple, in 1984. They gave him two premium payments totaling $1,712, which he allegedly deposited in his own bank account.

Fred Dougherty went to the hospital to see about having surgery performed, but was told that he was not insured. He repeatedly called Kontax, according to police, but was stalled in each instance by the saleman's assurance that there was a holdup at the main office. Eventually Dougherty reported the problem to the district attorney's office, and an investigation was launched.

Kontax has also admitted selling policies to an elderly woman in Smyrna and to another woman in Nashville. The insurance company honored the policy sold to the elderly woman although Kontax had not forwarded her premium payment, and Kontax later made restitution to the company, according to investigators.

The Tennessee Bureau (TBI) has also expressed the suspicion that Kontax may be the same man who, as an official of the State Blind Services Division, was suspended in 1977 for obtaining loans from blind vendors and getting them to cash personal checks for him which later bounced.

Investment Fraud

One federal source estimates that the amount of money raked in by so-called white-collar criminals from unsuspecting investors approaches what the underworld makes annually from the illegal drug deals. . . . That's about $80 billion. Tax shelter frauds alone are estimated to have drained $25 billion from the public and U.S. Treasury last year (1984).
—Connecticut Attorney General Joseph I. Leiberman
"Take Five," *Suburban News*

Phony investment scams are nothing new, but they never seem to go out of style. According to a recent survey conducted jointly by the North American Securities Administrators' Association and the Council of Better Business Bureaus, the Ponzi scheme (more popularly known as the pyramid scam) is now the number one fraud threat facing American investors. The survey shows that thousands of Americans nationwide were bilked out of $7.5 million through Ponzi schemes from 1982 to 1985, and the trend continues.

In a Ponzi scheme—also called a house of cards, endless chain, or Peter-Paul scheme—the investor's money is never actually invested by the promoter. He simply pays his clients "interest" by skimming funds from the payments of later investors, borrowing from Peter to pay Paul. Eventually the system collapses, and investors wake up to the fact that they have been duped. Initial investors frequently do receive a large return on their investments. This is an important part of the plan, because their enthusiastic recommendations to friends help to build the promoter's clientele. Later investors do not receive a return on their investments, however, and no participants get their capital back.

Other investment scams don't pay investors anything, but are merely fronts for taking in money. Such enterprises are of necessity short-lived, as the promoter who pays no interest finds it difficult to stall his clients when they start asking questions. He generally conducts a hit-and-run operation, whereby he collects his money and makes tracks.

While you can meet an investment scammer anywhere, unsolicited telephone calls are the most frequent source of consumer victimization, according to the Colorado Department of Regulatory Agencies, Division of Securities. Boiler-room operators buy lists of names and telephone numbers from credit-card companies, stockbrokers, and other sources, or call you if you respond to a newspaper advertisement or one that's been mailed to you.

Some legitimate companies do solicit business over the phone, but it is extremely risky to make an investment on the basis of a telephone pitch. Beware of offers promising high-profit, low-risk investments; once-in-a-lifetime opportunities; guaranteed profits; and salespeople who urge you to act immediately in order to cash in. The goal of these pitchmen is to convince you to send the company between $1,000 and $10,000 following the phone call.

Any type of investment can be used in a scam. The old standbys, gold and diamond mines, are still popular with swindlers, as they have been for hundreds of years. Oil and gas lease scams have been going strong for several years. (In one recent case, sales pitches for oil leases were made over the phone, followed up by boiler-room operators from the same company posing as oil-company representatives interested in buying customers' leases. The leases, on Illinois farmland, were originally bought up by the company for an average of $3 per acre, then sold over the phone, using high-pressure tactics, for about $500 an acre.)

New inventions always appeal to investors. A few amazing contraptions that have been fraudulently promoted recently include a miraculous carburetor that can save millions of dollars on oil and gasoline, reputedly ignored for years by automobile manufacturers in league with the gas companies; a machine that converts old tires into oil; an electricity-generating machine that runs forever on its own; and a machine that uses electromagnetism to propel missiles.

Other popular investment deals pitched by boiler-room operators are generic drugs, foreign-currency transactions, commodities, high-tech stocks, speculative real estate, precious metals, coal, and agriculture and livestock.

Con artists who offer phony investment opportunities are traditionally an especially slippery, fast-talking lot. The following brief stories, taken from news clippings around the country, will give you an idea of what today's investor is up against.

*   *   *

A real estate wheeler-dealer, convicted of stealing $2 million from investors in nonexisting developments, was granted a respite before sentencing by a judge so that he could make restitution to investors. The display of remorse that so touched the judge was apparently short-lived. The wheeler-dealer called an old schoolmate who had not heard from him for twenty years (since he had been best man at the wheeler-dealer's wedding), and persuaded him to invest $35,000 cash in the same real estate scam with which he had swindled his other victims. The wheeler-dealer was caught several days later with a passport, $35,000 in traveler's checks, and a one-way ticket to London.

"I have no more sympathy for you," said the judge at the sentencing, and gave him eight years in prison.

*   *   *

A man sold shares in a phony business, promising $250 interest per month plus commissions. He paid investors their interest by check. Since the checks were written for more than the correct amount, he asked the investors to refund the difference in cash, about $400 per check. The investors did so, but later discovered that the checks they had received had been drawn on a previously closed account.

*   *   *

An independent film producer, convicted in 1982 of selling unregulated securities and selling securities by false representation, finagled twenty-four court continuances before his sentencing, which finally took place in 1985. The producer had sold 110 investors $1.4 million in securities in order to finance film and television projects involving a Christmas story about a teddy bear. He had already successfully produced a picture book and a television special about the little bear, but instead of making the promised film and tape, he spent investors' money on personal business expenses.

At the sentencing, the producer shared his chair with three teddy bears at all times; unmoved by the cuteness of this ploy the prosecutor said that the producer was "nothing but a con man" who showed "no remorse." The bears did not appear to influence the judge, either. The producer got six years. Outside the courtroom he complained of "shabby journalism," and vowed to expose the journalists who had covered his trial in a new movie.

*   *   *

A tax lawyer allegedly cheated investors, most of them doctors, out of $200,000 in a scam involving land-development companies. He and his wife were living in Fort Lauderdale, Florida and fighting extradition to Texas on fraud charges. According to the tax lawyer, he had $2 million in stocks and bonds stashed in a suitcase in the trunk of his car in preparation for a trip to Switzerland, where he hoped to establish a line of credit. Although he was involved in the extradition process, he said, he saw nothing unusual in making a trip to Zurich; it was all a part of his job as an international financier specializing in tax law. Unfortunately, he parked his car outside a friend's house while he and his wife stopped to pay a call, and the car was burglarized; the suitcase was stolen from the trunk. Now, whether he goes to prison or not, his investors will never receive restitution.

* * *

Another interesting tale was told by the promoter of a recently failed Marshall Islands chartered bank. This promoter had lured depositors to his bank with promises of high returns on investments in international programs involving precious metals. There would be no income taxes levied on profits, he said, so long as the money was kept in an offshore bank. Then one day, $12 million in bank assets disappeared with the promoter. The last communication investors had from him was a nice note explaining that he was trailing the missing fund to make good on depositors' accounts.

How can you be sure whether an investment company is legitimate? It is extremely difficult. The best way is to deal only with well-established, well-respected firms. You can research the company's reputation by contacting your local consumer-protection office, Better Business Bureau, and State Attorney General's office. Remember, though, that a clean slate with these organizations is not a guarantee of legitimacy. All it means is that there has not been a complaint filed against the company. It is also a good idea to verify the promoter's claims with your state securities division. Investment contracts should be registered with the state securities division as securities offerings. Ask for detailed information in writing from the promoter, and be skeptical of deals that can't be checked out in person. Also, be suspicious of promoters who are reluctant to let you cash in your gains, but instead urge you to reinvest your interest in the program.

The Golden Chain

To illustrate how the pyramid scam works, let's look at the golden chain (GC), a high-roller's chain letter that makes the rounds every few years. The GC looks very tempting when it is proposed, since it appeals to the universal desire to get something for nothing.

A friend approaches you with a wonderful opportunity: You can make a one-hundred-dollar investment, paying him half and mailing the other half—a fifty-dollar bill—to the first person on the twelve-name list he gives you. Then, you make two copies of the list and give one to each of two friends whom you interest in the deal. They, in turn, each give you fifty dollars, so that you immediately make back your original investment. Then just sit back and wait for the money to roll in!

Your friend's enthusiasm—and greed—are contagious, and you also want to help him out. This personal contact is an important aspect of a high-priced chain letter. Because members are not enlisted through the mail, the recruiter gets his money back in person. Therefore, your friend points out, there is little risk, especially if you hedge your bet by finding two recruits before you pay your $100. Also, he tells you, the chain is not illegal, because you do not use the U.S. mail to send a letter of solicitation, but only to send cash. (Most Ponzi schemes, from chain letters to sophisticated investment scams, are pitched by promoters to be legal, but they are not. Using the mails in any way for a pyramid scheme is against U.S. postal laws, and state laws against pyramiding apply to Ponzi money-making plans of all kinds, including chain letters.)

The person-to-person approach used to enlist people in the golden chain has the effect of quickly saturating an area; the potential *universe,* or population likely to join the program, is limited to certain professional, family or social groups within a given vicinity. But, according to the guy who recruited you, you're lucky! There are only five local people above you on the twelve-name list, so only five people in town are now participating in the golden chain. You are getting in on the ground floor—or, more correctly, at the top of the pyramid. Right?

Wrong. The fact that there are five locals on your list suggests that there may be many more in town. Those who enjoy the study of geneology will find this easy to understand, since the progression of the golden chain is exactly like that of a family tree—that is, if you assume that every family member in every generation always has two kids. Using the family-tree metaphor, let's say that you are tracing your descent from the first golden chain participant, whom we will call Ezra. He is at the top of the tree. Everyone below him on your list represents a forebear of yours who is a direct descendant of Ezra. Ezra's downline looks like a chain; he is the first link, and you are the sixth.

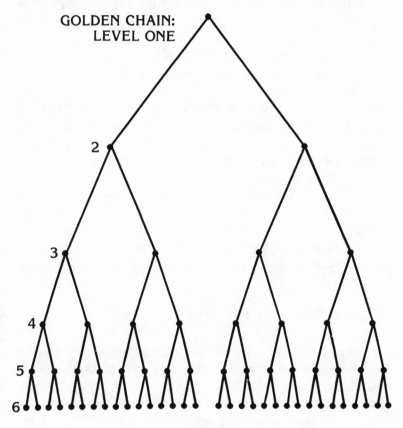

**GOLDEN CHAIN:
LEVEL ONE**

But remember—everyone in every generation of your family always has two kids. That means that in your generation there are thirty-two direct descendants of the old pioneer, each with his own chain. Including Ezra himself, there are not five, but as many as sixty-three local members of the family, spanning six generations.

Therefore, assuming that Ezra was the only person to introduce the golden chain to your town (although you really have no way of knowing whether others may also have recruited locally, establishing their own downlines), thirty-one other people are beating your time right now, trying to enlist your friends and neighbors before you can get to them to extract their fifty dollars.

By the time your name arrives at the top of the twelve-member list, you will theoretically rake in $32,769 from the people in your downline. In a pyramid scheme, gleaning the highest possible amount of money from a chain is called *achieving perfection*. The chain has now passed through twenty-four levels, from the top of the list to you, and so 4,194,312 people have participated, roughly the same number as the population of Maryland. Of course, if the guy at the top of your list was not the originator of the golden chain, the figure will be much higher. As you can see, achieving perfection is no easier in a pyramid scheme than in any other endeavor.

It is easy to see that the promotion of a pyramid scheme can be misleading to investors. Promoters rely on herd instinct and greed to further their scams, confident that most recruits to their programs won't see through the dazzling promise of money for nothing.

Multi-Level Marketing

In a distributorship, or multi-level, company, commissions and bonuses are earned according to the volume of your downline, the number of distributors working under you. In order to join the company, you must pay a fee. You are then authorized to recruit new people, each of whom pays you a certain percentage of his fee. When he in turn signs up new distributors, a smaller percentage of their fees will also go to you. This may continue for several levels.

Such businesses are not always pyramid schemes, nor is multi-level marketing a new concept. Mary Kay, Amway, and Herbalife are three examples of multi-level companies that have been in business for years—although the legality of Amway's operation has been questioned by the Federal Trade Commission and Herbalife has been sued for pyramiding by the State of California. The FTC dropped charges against Amway, and, as of this writing, the Herbalife trial is still in progress.

When is a multi-level, or distributorship, a pyramid operation? According to California Deputy Attorney General Michael Botwin, the answer to one simple question will tell you: Do you make money by recruiting or by selling? If the answer is *recruiting,* the business is a Ponzi, pyramid, or endless chain scheme, and is as such illegal.

When profits are made primarily through recruitment of new members rather than through product sales, the program works like a chain letter, and usually breaks down at the third level, when it becomes impossible to find new distributors to sign up. The people at the top of the pyramid do just fine, but it is usually impossible to tell at which level you are entering the program. And, as with any other kind of Ponzi scheme, there are built-in victims—the necessary people at the bottom of the heap, who pay off those at the top but receive no renumeration themselves.

Fraudulent multi-levels seem to crop up in three-year cycles, but their number has been increasing in recent years, especially in Los Angeles and Florida. Idaho has also been a hangout for pyramid promoters since 1981 when the state legislature eliminated enforcement of the state's consumer protection act.

A company may appear to be legitimate because it operates right out in the open and is tolerated by law-enforcement agencies, but state attorney general's offices and the FTC do not check out every multi-level company until there have been complaints filed, and people are not likely to start complaining until the chain has broken down.

Multi-level marketing companies operate across the United States, peddling such diverse products as automotive parts, cosmetics, detergents, and cures for arthritis, cancer, and multiple sclerosis. If you are interested in becoming a distributor for one of these businesses, watch for inflated claims that sound too good to be true, and ask yourself whether profits are to come from product sales or recruitment. Many illegal distributorship operations are secretive, with meetings conducted in private homes. Participants are encouraged to bring friends, family, and business associates into the plan. At the same time, promoters are always quick to assure potential recruits that the enterprise is legal. Be careful—it is illegal to participate in a pyramid scheme. And besides, you may lose your shirt.

Financial Planners

A final warning: financial planning is an expanding industry that provides a cover for swindlers and con artists. Financial planners provide a master plan for all aspects of an investor's finances. All states currently require broker-dealers to pass competency tests, and securities regulations in thirty-seven states call for registration of investment advisers; financial planners, however, are not required to meet industry-wide licensing and testing standards. The survey of the North American Securities Administrators Association and the Council of Better Business Bureaus, mentioned above, shows that hundreds of swindlers calling themselves financial planners used abusive tax shelters, Ponzi schemes, phony real-estate partnerships and other rip-offs to fleece investors.

After the Bone Marrow, Too

The eighties have brought hard times for many farmers, who faced bankruptcy and foreclosure as a result of low crop prices. When local banks, the courts, and the federal Farm Credit System failed to help, farm families were forced to try any solution that might offer a little hope. Into this dismal scenario, enter the con artist.

"All successful con artists tend to pick on any desperate group, and the most vulnerable people right now are farmers," said Charles Scholz, an assistant attorney general in Illinois. He knows what he's talking about.

One such swindler called a meeting at a Jacksonville, Illinois, hotel to offer advance-fee loans to farmers (loans for which a "finder's fee" is payable up front), according to Scholz. The swindler claimed to have "secret Arab sources" who wanted to invest in the American heartland. Like many another advance-fee loan shark, he took the farmers' loan-finding fees and ran, leaving his victims more desperate than before. One of the men who was taken in by the scam later said that he had believed the stranger because he quoted from the Bible.

*   *   *

There is an American folk saying, "the Devil can quote scripture," and it was probably inspired by Bible-thumping con artists. The strong religious convictions of America's rural population have frequently been played upon by swindlers over the generations, and with great success. Stuart A. McCreary, a minister of the Zion Christian Church in Zion, Illinois, was convicted in 1985 of participating in a fraudulent loan-finding scheme. Seventy farmers, ranging from an Oklahoma rancher to owners of very small farms, were cheated out of $1.25 million. Not easily disillusioned, McCreary's loyal congregation put the chapel up for his bail after he was arrested. He was sentenced to three years in prison and five years of probation and ordered to pay $40,000 restitution. His church is no longer active. Even on the day of sentencing, some farmers still hoped to get their loans.

*   *   *

Many farmers also fell for the advance-fee loan scam of Nasib Ed Kalliel, a Texan who sported a diamond ring and traveled the farm belt in a charter plane. Victims say that he played upon their feelings of anger against the Federal Land Bank and the Farmers' Home Administration—agencies responsible for many foreclosures—by promising to file class-action suits against the agencies. Kalliel and his company, First Financial Guaranty Corp., lost a suit filed by the Kansas attorney general, and were assessed $172,000 in civil penalties on charges of violating the Kansas Consumer Protection Act and the Kansas Corporate Farming Act.

Other suits have been brought against Kalliel by the State of Iowa, private individuals, and the Federal Deposit Insurance Corporation.

Kalliel had promised to assume farmers' debts and guarantee new loans in return for an 80 percent interest in their farms and a lease on improvements on their property. Farmers were offered living expenses and half the farm's profits; Kalliel also said he would create a vast agricultural network to allow farmers to buy supplies at minimum cost and to market grain abroad at premium prices.

Of course, like any other con artist, Kalliel had told audiences across the American heartland exactly what they wanted to hear. Many still have faith that, left on his own, he would have brought these dreams to fruition, and they blame the government for preventing him from carrying out his grand plan.

Says Missouri Director of Agriculture Charles E. Kruse, "It's unbelievable that anyone would take advantage of a situation such as the farm crisis and try to profit from it. . . . You'd think a vulture would move on after picking the bone clean. It now appears they're after the bone marrow, too."

Feelin' Great

Glen Wesley Turner, the granddaddy of distributorship pyramiding, made millions during the Seventies. He drew huge audiences, whipped them into a frenzy using evangelical techniques, and sent them out to recruit. By creating numerous franchises, he managed to operate for years until the law finally brought him down. Turner has the unique distinction of having legal actions filed against him by the FTC and the Securities and Exchange Commission (SEC), as well as being charged with fraud in all fifty states (though he never did go to prison). At one point, at least 1,500 distributors brought suit against Turner.

Turner may be out of business, but his legacy remains. Feelin' Great, a Florida-based company that markets its program in several states, describes Turner in its literature as "one of the country's top motivational speakers," whose "philosophy has changed the lives of thousands of people worldwide and turned dreams into reality." During Feelin' Great seminars, according to witnesses, audiences clap hands and chant from a script. One of the cheers used to build excitement goes, "If you want to make some money, clap your hands." This is reminiscent of Turner's chant "Go-go-go-Mmmmoney!"

It costs $80 to attend an introductory Feelin' Great seminar, where you can learn how to make money marketing a program called The Four Steps to Greatness. A pamphlet for one of the steps was written by none other than Glen W. Turner. The four-step program is pitched to seminar audiences for the price of $6,000. Buyers receive inspirational tapes, workbooks, and books and attend forty-eight hours of lectures and workshops.

Those who attend the introductory workshop are also given the opportunity to market the four steps to earn commissions. A marketer must sell $10,000 worth of programs in order to start earning his commission; after that he gets 30 percent of all his sales, as well as 10 percent of sales brought in by any new recruit he brings into the program.

Following a police raid on a seminar in Provo in September 1985, Feelin' Great has been restrained from operating in Utah until a civil case filed against the company by the state has been decided on its own merits. The company is charged with operating a pyramid scheme. Feelin' Great promoters also falsely told buyers that the four-step program had been endorsed by the Utah attorney general and the Church of Jesus Christ of Latter-Day Saints, according to the suit. (Because Utah has a heavily Mormon population, may scammers over the years have either obtained church support under false pretenses or have pretended to have church endorsement as a means to draw the faithful into their webs.)

Lawsuits in Tennessee and Texas have also barred the

company from operating. Lawyers for Feelin' Great deny that the company is a pyramid scheme. Furthermore, they say, the fact that Turner's name is used in their program does not automatically incriminate the company.

James S. Barker, an assistant Utah attorney general, believes that members of Feelin' Great are really paying for the chance to get other people into the program and not for forty-eight hours of instruction.

"If these people wanted education, they could spend that money to go to Brigham Young University and get a bachelor's degree," he said.

Richard Johnson, a Feelin' Great defense attorney in Utah, maintains that the only people who became dissatisfied with the company were those who had used poor business judgment in borrowing money in order to buy into the program, according to Salt Lake City's *Deseret News*.

All that Glitters: Three Scams

His only known employment was as a convenience store clerk in Fort Lauderdale, but Nelson F. Radabaugh—or Charles J. Hecker, as he was known in Florida—described himself in a slick brochure as a world-renowned architect, an intensely humanitarian prison reformer, and a financial whiz. According to Fort Lauderdale police detective Stephen Raabe, "He was one of these people who had a gift of gab."

Radabaugh's brochure also stated that he was able to get gold at below-market prices from a friend with a mysterious gold mine in Nevada. He offered potential investors interest of 10 percent a month, and at least 110 Floridians, some of them doctors and lawyers, sank approximately $1.5 million in the nonexistent mine, Raabe said.

Radabaugh allegedly began operating his scam in Miami during the late Seventies, moved his operation to Fort Lauderdale in 1980, and then fled to San Diego, California, in 1983 when he realized the police were on his trail.

In California, Radabaugh continued his gold-mine scheme, taking in a total of $2.5 million from about 100 investors. In October 1984 he was arrested in San Diego on a Florida grand-theft warrant; soon afterward, the State of California realized it had its own case against him. In July 1985 he pleaded guilty to ten of the sixty-one counts brought against him in San Diego, receiving a sentence of eight years in prison. Radabaugh, 62, also faces extradition to Florida, where he is expected to stand trial for grand theft.

*   *   *

Gold-scam con artist Richard Whitehurst, who had already served time for selling nonexistent bullion in Northern California, was given a seven-year suspended prison sentence and placed on five years' probation by a U.S. district court judge in Los Angeles in mid 1985. He was also ordered to do 6,000 hours of community work, possibly including counseling for the NAACP, fined $12,000, and ordered to make $40,000 restitution to two brothers from Utah, one a gold miner and the other a dentist, whom he had pleaded guilty of cheating.

With the plea, charges stemming from a suspected one-million-dollar scam were dropped. The $1 million was allegedly taken from a group of Southern California and Mexican business men who, like the men from Utah, believed that they were investing in gold.

Assistant U.S. Attorney Mike Emmick has called the sentence a travesty. He said that perhaps Judge A. Andrew Houk believed Whitehurst's "ludicrous" claim that he was a sort of modern-day Robin Hood, who stole only from drug dealers trying to launder money by buying gold.

"None of the victims here or in Los Angeles are drug dealers," Emmick stated in a letter to the judge. "He could have brought the Robin Hood story to other sentencing judges but didn't. He just thought it up now."

*   *   *

A fifty-two-year old woman who owns a mobile home and trailer park might not seem like your average con artist. But Lena Elmendorf, arrested in early 1985 on numerous charges, pleaded guilty to one count of second-degree grand larceny and has been indicted on one count of extortion.

In 1982 she convinced investors to place $40,000 in a non-existent gold-and-silver mining company called J. Q. Enterprises, which she said was located in Valdor, Canada. Elmendorf admitted that there was no such company, and agreed to make restitution.

The indictment also involved an alleged plot in which a Hyde Park, New York, businessman was told by Elmendorf that there was a contract out on his son by organized crime members in Columbia County. She allegedly told the man that his son would be killed unless the contract was canceled, and offered to negotiate the cancellation for $25,000.

State troopers have said that the man made two ten-thousand-dollar payments before going to the police, who supplied him with $3,000 to make another payment. This one, troopers claim, was witnessed by law-enforcement authorities. The contract, like the mining company, never existed.

At this writing Elmendorf is awaiting sentencing. According to a district attorney presiding in the case, she could receive a combination of jail time and probation and be ordered to make financial restitution.

Vacondo Debacle

Hersch Caudill was described by his former classmates at the University of Florida as a genius at tax law. He graduated first in his tax-law class and also had a degree in accounting. Described as a pleasant, cooperative man by police investigators and reporters as well as friends, Caudill is not a person you'd expect to see mixed up in an operation like the Vacondo debacle. Yet, at thirty-eight, he pleaded guilty to charges of stealing $500,000 from investors in Vacondo, a time-share investment operation based in Orlando, Florida. At Caudill's sentencing in September 1984, the judge asked him what happened.

"It was a combination of first, some financial debts, then greed, and then, I think it was just sort of a feeling that everything would turn out all right," Caudill answered.

"When you deviate a little bit, you start sinking deeper and deeper. That was what happened to me."

Hersch Caudill went to work for Vincent Cremata, 52, Eric McGrew, 38, and Norman Peires, also 38, as a tax lawyer for Vacondo in March 1983. At first, he said, he believed that Vacondo would work as a tax-sheltered investment company; it was not until later that he realized that the basic plan was faulty, involving violations of securities and tax laws that would invalidate the huge tax exemptions that made Vacondo attractive to investors.

According to investigators, one of the basic violations was that Vacondo was composed of three companies that were interrelated. For investments to be tax-exempt, the companies would have had to be independent of one another.

The first company was run by a retired physician named Victor Cremata, who organized tax seminars around the country for doctors and dentists. The tax seminars directed interested clients to Eric McGrew's investment counseling company, where they were advised to put their money in Vacondo.

While Cremata, McGrew, and Peires all claimed that their companies were independent, investigators say that they all worked together. All three companies had offices on the twelfth floor of the CNA Tower in downtown Orlando.

Caudill testified that his illegal involvement with Vacondo started in May, when Cremata, McGrew, and Peires asked him to siphon $170,000 from the three Vacondo escrow accounts which Caudill controlled. The funds were needed, they explained, for personal and business expenses—including Caudill's law bill.

Caudill explained that to remove money from the accounts would be illegal. The three still wanted to siphon the money, Caudill said, "even though they knew and I knew it was illegal. That's when I first knew that I was a conspirator in this thing and not a counsel."

At this time he still believed that Vacondo would be a success, and that the money could be paid back later, he said.

About six weeks before the actual breakup of Vacondo,

Peires and McGrew began to feud. Peires composed an inflammatory letter and sent it out to all Vacondo investors, accusing McGrew of making improper advances of more than half a million dollars of investors' money. Warning recipients of the letter that "much is wrong with the company," he threatened to bring suit against McGrew. If he were to do so, he said, regulatory agencies would "turn the company inside-out," and the result would be a "mini-Hiroshima."

Not to be outdone, McGrew struck back a week later, turning the tables on Peires by suing him first. Peires had not only withheld information about his criminal past in South Africa, said McGrew, but he also intended to "loot and convert to his own use" investors' money. Peires, the suit charged, had already looted and converted more than $150,000. After a week or so of such colorful invective, McGrew dismissed the suit. By that time Vacondo was already done for.

Employees had reported to police their suspicions that the whole tax-shelter scheme was nothing more than a high-priced fraud, and an investigation was launched. In late September 1984, Vacondo officials prepared for a $200 million public-investment offering. Caudill was, by his own account, frightened by the role he had played in a scheme that he now clearly saw had been a complete fraud from its inception. In early October he headed out.

He didn't tell his wife he was leaving until the day he split. Traveling by plane and bus, Caudill went to Ohio, California, and Texas. For a while he operated a successful lawn-mowing business in San Antonio.

Meanwhile, police investigators had sued Vacondo to close it down, and, with the help of comptroller's officials, had confiscated boxes containing thousands of documents from its offices. Caudill contacted law-enforcement officials, worked out a plea deal with prosecutors, and came back to Orlando almost a year after he had left, coordinating his return with the arrest of his old friends Cremata, McGrew, and Peires on racketeering and fraud charges. Caudill has agreed to testify for the state at their trial in the $1.7 million case as part of his prior agreement with prosecutors, and spent several weeks helping prosecutors sort out Vacondo documents as part of a work-release program.

What does the defense have to say about Caudill? Cremata's lawyer was not shy about stating his opinion. "Hersch Caudill got a sweetheart deal," he said. "I saw him the other day walking downtown, and he's wearing a coat and tie; he doesn't have anybody watching him. That's better than the average guy gets for stealing a half million and screwing up a company so a bunch of investors lose their money."

When Caudill was convicted and was given a five-year jail term, he was forbidden to practice accounting, law, or real-estate brokerage ever again, and agreed to repay $350,000 in income taxes for the money he stole. Although he admitted to stealing $500,000 from Vacondo, Caudill swore that he had only $5,500 left when he fled Orlando in September 1984. The rest, he said, had been spent on sports cars, debts, and real estate.

"If they want to make it look like a cushy deal, so be it," said one investigator. "But his sentence is five years, and when he gets out, he's walking out of jail stripped of any way to make a living."

Resort to Fraud

It's hard to know who to trust these days, but thirty Floridians felt that it was safe to put their faith in Fred "Holy" Walters, a forty-seven-year-old Orlando developer and former Baptist preacher. Not only did they put their faith in Walters, they also made another mistake; they put their savings in his hands.

You can't really call a person dumb for assuming that an investment in a Christian resort development for Southwest Orange County would be on the up-and-up. Walters is charged with bilking the thirty investors out of more than $1 million, as well as bribing a loan officer at Flagship Bank in East Orlando. Walters allegedly gave her $20,000 as an inducement to grant him $525,000 in improper loans.

The head of the loan department met with Walters when

he discovered the loans, and said that Walters promised to pay them back. He did not do so, however, according to the bank's records, and the money was eventually written off as a bad debt.

Walters has admitted to paying the loan officer for the loans, but his attorney told jurors at his trial before Orange County Circuit Court that it was the loan officer, not Walters, who broke the law.

At this writing, the loan officer has been fired, the investors are still out $1 million, and Walters' guilt or innocence has not yet been decided by the Court.

Self-Styled Financial Advisor

Victor Mullen was well known and well liked in Rosell, Illinois. There was nothing pushy or pretentious about this self-styled financial advisor. He would just mention, in passing, that he had some pretty fair investment opportunities that would return interest at the rates of 18 to 60 percent. He never used a hard-sell approach, and he didn't go out of his way to meet people.

Friendships came easily to Mullen; it seemed everyone in town invested with him, from the school superintendent to local truckers. Involved in the community's school, church, business, and social life, Mullen liked to talk about his kids and his church, but he was never preachy or pedantic. He didn't seem stuck up about his good looks or the knack he had for making money, either. His business phone was an answering service; his secretary was his wife.

Mullen's main investment plan was to purchase used medical equipment at auctions in St. Louis and Atlanta, and then to resell the equipment at a profit. He offered high returns, but insisted on a minimum $10,000 investment.

One investor, a warehouse worker, was skeptical at first. He met Mullen at a party, listened to his low-key pitch, and then waited for a year. When he asked friends and neighbors who had invested with Mullen, they told him that they were receiving the interest that had been promised.

Like many other investors, the warehouse worker got cash advances on credit cards, took out a second mortgage on his home, and took his savings out of the bank so that he could get in on the deal. Each month, Mullen would give investors just enough to pay off the credit-card advances; he encouraged his friends and neighbors to reinvest the interest they earned rather than collect on it.

Another investor was a high school gym teacher who met Mullen through an over-thirty basketball club that Mullen had organized. The gym teacher invested $60,000 from seven credit cards, a second mortgage, and a savings account. Mullen gave him promissory notes guaranteeing that the money would be repaid at several interest rates, going as high as 60 percent. The gym teacher said that at one time he wanted to take out part of his money, but that Mullen discouraged it. It could be done, the investment counselor said, but it would have to come out of his own pocket, and it would be a hardship for him. If he did return the money, he said, he would never do business with the gym teacher again. The teacher backed down.

"We were all living in a fool's paradise, I guess, until Victor died," said another investor, a woman who had met Mullen through her church. "We still can't believe that he shot himself. He seemed very happy. We were too, till we realized that he was dead and our money was kaput, too."

On a hunting expedition at an exclusive South Texas game preserve in July 1984, Mullen shot himself through the chest with his shotgun, according to reports. For several years prior to his death, Mullen had been making payments of $24,600 a year on several insurance policies. At the time of his death, his wife collected $4.3 million from the policies. This money was the only asset left by Victor Mullen. There never had been any investments; there had never been any medical equipment. For ten years Mullen had apparently been running a well-organized Ponzi scheme in Roseville.

When the house of cards collapsed, more than 100 Roseville residents lost everything, and 102 of them are bringing suit against Mullen's wife and the estate for reimbursement of $3.8 million.

Maxim Winters, Mrs. Mullen's lawyer, has called the federal racketeering suit "a fruitless attempt by people motivated by greed to separate a grieving widow from her rightful insurance money." Whether or not Victor Mullen's business practices were legal, Winters asserts—and he professes ignorance in this area—the insurance money cannot legally be taken from Shelly Mullen.

Investors claim that, as secretary of the operation, Shelly Mullen must have been a party to the scheme perpetrated by her husband. Besides, they say, it was their money that paid for those insurance policies.

At this writing, the court battle is still raging. According to Winters, "The question here is, can these people take away a widow's insurance money?"

"Financial Humpty-Dumpty"

In August 1985, a federal grand jury in Orlando, Florida, indicted Alexander William Herbage, an Englishman, on twenty-three counts of mail fraud and two counts of interstate transportation of property obtained by fraud. He is accused of bilking more than 3,000 U.S. investors of more than $46 million. If Herbage were to be convicted on all twenty-five counts, he could receive a 135-year prison sentence. But he will have to be extradited first.

At this writing, Herbage is confined in a jail hospital in Winchester, England, where he is being held without bail on charges that he filed false financial statements with creditors. At 500 pounds, he is too large for an ordinary cell. He is also too large for a uniform, and so he wears a dressing gown. Herbage, dubbed the "financial Humpty-Dumpty" by *Barron's* business journal, sleeps in a reinforced bed.

Before his fall, Herbage presented a very attractive picture to investors in England, the Netherlands, and the United States. His right-wing political views were soothing to many who were looking for a safe place to put their money. An outspoken advocate of Margaret Thatcher's policies and a foe of Communists, Herbage published photos of himself

with members of the English royalty in his weekly financial newsletter. With money gleaned from investors starting
in 1978, Herbage bought his home, a country manor in Sut-
ton, England, patrolled by thirty-seven guards and grazed
by a herd of longhorn steers. He owned villas in the South
of France and a house in the Netherlands, and leased an
apartment in Paris; he chartered private jets and collected
art work by Picasso, Miro, Seurat, and Henry Moore. With
so much style, and so much wealth to support it, minor
eccentricities like his weight, his habit of drinking gallons
of milk daily, and his nonstop conversation were more a
plus than a minus in the eyes of many of his investors. After
all, you'd expect a well-heeled English gentleman to be
colorful.

Billing himself as a sophisticated international financial
advisor and commodities and currency expert, Herbage
advertised three funds, known as the Caprimex Group, in
mailings sent out across the United States. The *Duck Book,*
a finanical newsletter of the "doom and gloom" school of
economic forecasting, also carried information on Caprimex.
Many people who were worried about the economic collapse
of the nation decided to trust Alex Herbage with their
savings. Herbage, often requiring minimum deposits
ranging from $10,000 to $35,000, promised dividends up
to 35 percent.

The message seemed to be that yes, the world is going
to hell in a handbasket, but here is a man who knows what
to do with money. The manor, guards, royal guests, anti-
Communist think-tank hosted by Herbage and promoted
as a medieval feasting—all of these suggested stability to
American investors.

Pity the poor colonists, most of them Floridians, who
imagined the scenes of merry olde England, as painted by
Alex Herbage, to be more solid, more dependable, than the
plastic and glitz all around them. They could have invested
in McDonald's. Instead, they put their faith in the pretend
world of Alex Herbage, and many of them lost thousands
of dollars.

Herbage's glory days were between 1978, when he started

the Caprimex companies, and 1984, when the illusions he so skillfully crafted were destroyed. Before that period, he failed in several enterprises, including a twist parlor (disco) called the Checkerboard Club in London, an International Commodities Corp., in Panama which lost investors $15 million, and a supermarket in Gibralter. The Caprimex group was a masterpiece, but it lasted only until investors and some of his own sales representatives started getting huffy about demanding refunds. In early 1985 the BBC showed a videotape of Herbage on a sidewalk in London as a Dutch investor overtook him and beat him up. According to the report of his jailer, who saw the scene on the telly, the fat man resembled "a large beetle, rolling around on the pavement, that couldn't get up."

The lord of the manor is reduced to a beetle; so much for the tricks and contrivances of con artists. The man who forecast the fall of the U.S. economic system has watched his own financial empire collapse.

It is possible that U.S. investors may recoup some of their losses, when and if Alexander is extradited to Orlando, and if he is convicted of fraud.

Ronald Rewald and the CIA

"I had a client who lost a hundred thousand in a real-estate swindle. I advised against getting into it and he said, 'But look who's investing,' and named a very prominent local businessman. It turned out the name that lent so much assurance to this very shaky development was part of the scheme and the investors lost nine million dollars."

Stick said, "Without having to point a gun at anybody."

"You go to the same prison though," Kyle said.

—Elmore Leonard
Stick

Bishop, Baldwin, Dillingham and Wong, Ronald Rewald's Hawaii-based investment firm, was forced into bankruptcy by angry investors in July 1983. In August, Rewald unsuccessfully attempted suicide by slitting his wrists. In October 1985, after an eleven-week trial involving 150 witnesses and 2,000 exhibits, he was found guilty of ninety-four felony counts of fraud, perjury, and embezzlement and faces a prison term of 400 years. Federal prosecutors said that Rewald had swindled more than 400 investors out of $20.6 million in a pyramid scheme. Ten million were used to pay back investors in principal and bogus interest; $5 million went to maintain a lavish corporate facade, reeking of affluence and stability; and Rewald used the rest of the money to maintain his extravagant lifestyle.

Rewald's defense was that the CIA set up and ran his company. No, Bishop, Baldwin was not a real investment company, he admitted; yes, he took millions of dollars from investors; but it was all done in the interests of the Agency.

CIA officials admit using Bishop, Baldwin as "light cover" for agents and as a telephone and telex backstop, but have denied any part in the fraud. Several agents invested in the company, and all of them lost money, according to court records.

According to Rewald, CIA involvement went far deeper; in fact, he claimed he was forced to spend investors' money on polo ponies, cars, houses, ranches, women, art and antique weapons in order to keep up appearances. The Agency demanded it of him. The real business of Bishop, Baldwin, he insisted, was dealing in military arms with Taiwan. The government contends that no such deal ever went through. Rewald claims that, had the arms deal gone as originally planned by the Agency, $10 million would have been generated to pay back the investors. Rewald was instructed by the CIA to use the investors' money to befriend the Sultan of Brunei, the Filipino business executive Enrique Zobel, and other influential international figures.

The defense also maintained that Rewald's phony Marquette University diploma was provided by the CIA. This was considered a low blow by the Agency. The document was a transparent fake, testified a CIA expert, and had clearly been produced by a rank amateur.

About 150 pieces of information relating to the CIA were recovered from Bishop, Baldwin after the business was taken over by a legal trustee during the summer of 1983. These documents were placed under seal by the bankruptcy court at the request of the CIA and were reviewed by CIA officials in private. Despite the requests made by the defense, Judge Harold Fong refused to change his order to bar most of the CIA-related information from testimony. Throughout the trial, Fong held that only information showing CIA authorization or control of funds spent by Bishop, Baldwin was relevant and therefore admissable.

Federal public defender Michael Levine disagreed with the judge's decision to bar CIA-related information. His client, he said, was not trying to get permission to reveal anything that would endanger national security; preventing Rewald from giving the complete story was, he said, inherently unfair.

"It's as if you asked someone to recite the alphabet to prove he knows it. And he says, 'Sure I know it: A, Q, T, and Z.' You'd laugh at him. Rewald has to be able to recite the entire alphabet. He can't be told that he can only refer to certain letters."

Whatever the extent of CIA involvement in Bishop, Baldwin may have been, Rewald was certainly capable of operating as a con artist without being coerced by the Agency. Before moving to Hawaii he was convicted of failing to register with the State of Wisconsin in a franchise operation, and of making untrue and misleading claims to investors. Even the name of the phony investment firm, devised by Rewald, was an obvious attempt at misrepresentation. Bishop, Baldwin and Dillingham are all *Kamaaina* families, nineteenth-century settlers of Hawaii still highly respected on the islands today. In a debate between a posturing con man given to flaunting elaborate falsehoods on one hand and an organization known for its compulsion to conceal everything that touches its operations on the other, the whole truth is not likely to be revealed.

Rewald's ability to put on a convincing show is revealed by the fact that Jack Lord, one-time star of the television series "Hawaii Five-O," was taken in by the imposter. The prosecution said that Rewald used the names of famous people, including the Kamaaina families, business and political figures, and Jack Lord, to create an illusion of substance.

Lord testified that he had become friends with Rewald, critiqued some movie ideas for him, and sold him his mobile dressing room from the television series for $45,000. He had not, however, knowingly lent his name to Rewald's business dealings. Asked by the prosecution why his name appeared on the firm's organization chart, Lord said it was because "Rewald put it there without my knowledge or consent."

The actor was unaware that one of the Bishop, Baldwin offices was referred to by staffers as "Jack Lord's office," nor did he know until the trial that his name had been painted on one of the company's reserved parking stalls.

"If (Rewald) had told anyone that I had occupied an office . . . it would have been a damnable lie," he said. "I hate to be used. Anyone hates to be used. I would have considered that being used."

When Lord turned in the witness seat to glare at Rewald in a manner reminiscent of his role as Steve McGarrett, chief of the Hawaii Five-O special police force, there were whispers throughout the courtroom of the line so often delivered by McGarrett to his sidekick: "Book him, Danno."

Lord testified that he had believed in Rewald's legitimacy in part because the offices of Bishop, Baldwin had been so luxurious. For a con artist dealing in phony investments, a lavishly appointed office is worth every penny it costs. Its carpeting, draperies, and furniture should look expensive and tasteful. It should sound busy, with ringing telephones, clattering typewriters, and the clicks, whirs, and beeps of computers. All in all, it should positively reek of money in the making. The phony investment scammer's office is essentially an elaborate stage set, designed to make investors feel so much confidence in the business they want to fork over their life savings. It is ironic that such a stage set should have fooled a veteran actor like Jack Lord.

It is also ironic that the trustee appointed to take over Bishop, Baldwin after its bankruptcy found no real assets belonging to the company other than the props used to lull investors into a false sense of security—the office furnishings.

Milk Mold Malarkey

Want to make big bucks as a culture farmer? Here's the deal. You send us $395, and we'll mail you a starter kit containing ten packets of lactic activator BC40 and a supply of foil envelopes. All you have to do is pour milk, grated cheddar cheese, and BC40 powder into your blender, switch it to mix, and then pour out the concoction into suitable containers. Mason jars will do fine.

Store the jars in your basement for only one week, and you're ready to harvest! Skim the yogurtlike substance off the top of the mixture in each jar, let it dry, and then fill your foil envelopes with the white, powdery milk mold. We will pay you from six to ten dollars for each envelope! You will make $900 from each $395 investment, or $20,480 in one year!

Why are we willing to pay so much for milk mold? Because, believe it or not, it is in great demand. You see, Cleopatra was the first to popularize milk-culture beauty products. The secret was lost for hundreds of years, until a woman living in Africa rediscovered the rejuvenating and beautifying properties of milk mold. People around her noticed that, while everyone else grew older looking, she seemed to grow younger with each passing year. Finally she was prevailed upon to share her miraculous find with the world! The House of Cleopatra Beauty Secret has begun production of a line of beauty preparations using this unique formula. Unfortunately, it is impossible to grow the primary ingredient—milk mold—in quantity using commercial methods.

That's where you come in. By culture farming right now in your own home, you will be producing a commodity for which there is a great demand. We will buy all you can produce!

*   *   *

If the proposition set forth above sounds good to you, you're in luck. You won't get a chance to fall for the lactic activists' pitch, because Culture Farms, Inc., was ordered closed in June 1985 by Shawnee County, Kansas, District Judge James Buchele, who ruled that the company was using an illegal investment contract.

At the time of its closing the company had been operating for just one year, yet at least 2,800 culture farmers in at least twenty states had paid between $80 million and $100 million for activator kits. About $10 million of investors' money is thought by authorities to have been diverted into the promoters' pockets. In August 1985 Culture Farms executives filed for reorganization under Chapter 11 of federal bankruptcy laws, but no culture farmer-investors were listed among the top twenty creditors.

In September 1985, following a six-month investigation by a joint federal and state task force, a federal grand jury in Topeka, Kansas, indicted twelve people involved with the scheme on sixty-three counts of mail fraud and one count of conspiracy on charges that they had been operating a pyramid scheme. The maximum sentence for these charges would be a five-year prison term and a fine of $10,000 for one count of conspiracy, and fine of $1,000 and five years' imprisonment for each count of mail fraud.

Most of those indicted were high-ranking officers in one or more of the companies created by Culture Farms, Inc.; Activator Supply, Nevada; Rontel Tele-Marketing Corp. of California; Diversified Labs, Inc., of Kansas; Kubus Nursery of Nevada; and House of Cleopatra's Secret, Nevada. Some of these may have been merely paper companies, invented for the sole purpose of diverting money. The House of Cleopatra's Secret did in fact produce a small quantity of milk-culture cosmetics, but these were used only as props at sales meetings. Actress Jane Powell was hired to plug the line of beauty products, but she was unaware of the true nature of the company, officials say. The indictment alleges that the only demand for the cultures was that created by the defendants for the purpose of inducing investors to buy activator kits. At least 90 percent of the milk mold sent in by culture farming investors was used to make activator kits for new investors. Payment for the cultures did not come from sales of Cleopatra's Secret beauty preparations, but from the fees paid by later investors.

While most of the Culture Farms promoters' pitch was pure malarkey, it is in a sense true that the secret formula for milk mold came to the United States by way of Africa. In the late 1970s, investors in the Republic of South Africa lost millions of dollars in a similar scam. Gert Theron, 46, one of the twelve indicted and a citizen of South Africa, is credited with starting the milk-farming scheme in the United States. Three other defendants also have foreign citizenships, although they have been residing in the United States: Terrence J. Taylor, 39, president of Culture Farms, Inc., is a British citizen; Christopher J. Mancuso, 27, vice president of marketing for culture farms, is a Canadian; and Frans Theron, 43, brother of Gert Theron, is also a South African.

Appendix A: Insurance Fraud Indicators

The following list is not complete, but is representative of the signs insurance crime-stoppers look for when they investigate claims.

Automobile Accident Fraud

Fraud may be indicated when claimant or insured is:
1. Overly eager for a speedy settlement.
2. Unusually eager to take the blame for an accident.
3. Exceptionally conversant with insurance, medical, or vehicle repair terminology.
4. Insistent that the claimant caused the accident. (The ICPI then suspects that the insured is playing along with a ring of crooks who stage accidents.)

General elements that may point to fraud:
1. A rental vehicle is involved in the accident.
2. The vehicle involved in the claim contains three or four unrelated people when it is struck.
3. The police report was not made at the scene of the accident, or there is no police report.
4. The accident happened soon after one or more of the vehicles involved was registered and insured; or a month or less before the policy was due to expire; or soon after insurance coverage was increased to include comprehensive and collision.
5. A post-office box or hotel is given as an address for one or more claimants.
6. The claimant shows an "active claim history."

Property damage fraud or inflation may be indicated when:

1. All of the vehicles involved in the accident are taken to the same shop to be repaired.
2. The accident is major, but there are no subjectively diagnosed injuries (see below, under medical fraud elements, for definition).
3. The collision is minor, but the repair costs are high.
4. Although the vehicle could not have been driven away from the scene of the accident according to the repair estimates, no towing charge is included in the claim.
5. Body-shop employees or owner discourage an insurance appraiser from looking at a vehicle involved in the accident.

Medical fraud may be suspected when:

1. All injuries are those called subjectively diagnosed, including headaches, whiplash, and muscle spasm.
2. The medical bills submitted are photocopies, especially third or fourth generation.
3. The collision is minor, but the injuries, especially subjectively diagnosed injuries, are excessive.
4. The medical bill submitted does not itemize office visits and treatments.

Lost earnings claims may be inflated when:

1. The submitted employment information is from a small business, especially a business with a post-office box as its address.
2. When the business phone number given in the claim is called, it is answered by an answering or secretarial service, or by a recording.
3. The claimant started the job just before the accident.
4. The statement of lost earnings is not typed up on company letterhead.
5. The lost earnings statement has elements that don't concur with other elements in the claim; for example, the income earned may not be appropriate to the neighborhood listed.

Arson

Coincidences at the time of the fire that may indicate arson:

1. The family that owns property is out of town when fire occurs.
2. Items that have sentimental or intrinsic value have apparently been removed from the building shortly before the fire.
3. The family pet is not present at the time of the burning of a home.

Fire fraud may be indicated if:

1. The building that burned was for sale.
2. The building was purchased recently.
3. The loss of a commercial property includes inventory that is unsaleable or banned by a government agency.
4. The insured has been having financial difficulty.
5. More than one person holds the mortgage on the property that burned.
6. The building is deteriorating or is located in a deteriorating neighborhood.

Indications of Ambulance Chasing or Personal Injury Mill Operations

1. The attorney's lien or representation letter is dated the same day as that on which the accident occurred.
2. The claimant develops subjectively diagnosed injuries only after he or she has consulted with a lawyer.
3. There are unrelated occupants in the vehicle involved in an accident, all of whom contract with the same lawyer or doctor.
4. The accident is minor, but medical and lost wages claims are major.
5. The doctor's bill and report for victims of different accidents do not substantially differ from one another.

6. Medical bills show that a patient received routine treatment on dates of weekends or holidays.
7. The same doctor and lawyer handle major medical and lost earnings claims regularly, as if they were working hand-in-glove.

Appendix B: Hanging Bad Paper

The U.S. Federal Reserve Bank handles about 400,000 bad checks on an average day, but the daily rate is significantly higher during October through January. FBI statistics indicate that about 70 percent of all white-collar crime occurs during this holiday season, including credit card fraud, embezzlement, and various kinds of employee theft.

Most bad checks are passed by amateurs; about half of all checks drawn on insufficient funds are the result of checkbook errors. Major department store owners have found that an overwhelming majority of such checks are on new accounts and are numbered between 101 and 200. Some bank officials deduce that about 75 percent of those who write bad checks do so repeatedly, and that those who are basically honest folk tend to write bad checks for necessities, while intentional defrauders go for cash.

Checks drawn on accounts with insufficient funds to cover them are hot checks, and may or may not be written intentionally to defraud. With a forged check however, the intent to defraud is clear. Sophisticated techniques are used to produce such checks on color-copying machines, and check-writing machines are also employed in this process. Forgers use old checks or letterheads, or cut logos from advertisements. These are pasted up on a blank or stolen check to serve as a layout. The layout will be photocopied to produce the checks that the paper hangers will attempt to pass.

First, though, the forger must add routing and account

numbers to the bottom of the check, or change the numbers that are already there. The series of numbers inside the brackets at the bottom of the check indicate the Federal Reserve District Bank with which the issuing bank is affiliated. There are twelve district banks across the country, numbered from east to west. New York, for example, is coded 02, while California is coded 12.

The third digit refers to the Federal Reserve branch, the fourth digit to the clearinghouse, and the last five digits are the bank's identification number. (For savings and loans banks, add 20 to the first two digits.)

In most forgeries, the first two digits will be wrong. This gives the check-passer time, as the check will be routed to the Federal Reserve bank indicated by the digits. The check appears to be written on a local New York bank, for example, so the teller explains that there must be a three-day waiting period, giving the check time to clear, before money can be withdrawn from an account. The passer waits three or four days and withdraws his money with no one the wiser, since he routed the check to California; it will be days yet before the bank realizes that the check is bad.

U.S. NATIONAL, INC. _____19___	2110
PAY TO THE ORDER OF _____	\$ _____
_____	DOLLARS
FOR _____	
⑆301073183⑆ 50 133331⑈	

Authentic routing numbers are printed with magnetic ink, but the forger uses regular printer's ink. Distribution of magnetic ink is tightly controlled, but the forger usually prefers plain old black ink anyway. Why? Because routing computers cannot read it. His check will be hand-routed, occasioning a processing delay, which from his point of view is all to the good.

Counterfeit checks are cut with a paper cutter and the numbers in the upper right-hand corner are added. These will be high, to indicate that the account is an old, well-established one.

How to spot a forgery? First look at the digits at the bottom of the check. Are they shiny? If so, they are not printed in magnetic ink. Look at the routing number to see whether it corresponds with the bank the check is written on. If the bank is First National of Rhode Island, for example, but the routing number is 11 (Texas), then there's a problem! You need not know all of the Federal Reserve district bank codes to see that the number must be wrong, as the Eastern banks have the lowest numbers.

Also, look for perforations. Real checks almost always tear along a perforated line, while forged checks seldom do.

The check number is usually typed in or stamped on a forged check; a press that does consecutive printing is another expensive item that the run-of-the-mill forger has difficulty getting his hands on.

Date-coding is used in many branch banks to show when an account was opened. The number 728535, for example, decoded, means July 2, 1985, branch 35. Different banks will put this code in different places on the check. If this number does not jibe with the check number in the upper right-hand corner—the date code indicates that the account was opened two months ago, but the check is numbered 1003, for example—this should be a warning signal.

Kiting

Check-kiting can be extremely profitable and is a favorite of the business-oriented con man. Kiting is often practiced by investment swindlers, who kite in order to look good on paper, with an artificially inflated bank account, as well as to be able to withdraw and use large sums of money they don't actually have.

Here's how kiting works: Mr. A opens a checking account in Akron, Ohio, using a $250 check drawn on a bank in

Buffalo, New York, as an initial deposit. At the time he deposits this check, there is no money in the Buffalo account to back it up.

Next day, either Mr. A or his business partner, Mr. B, deposits a check drawn on the Akron account in the Buffalo account. When the check used to establish the Akron account arrives in Buffalo, it will be covered.

On the third day, Mr. A deposits a check at the Akron bank. It is for $400, drawn on the Buffalo bank.

On the fourth day, Mr. A or Mr. B writes a $500 check on the Akron account and deposits it in the Buffalo account.

In four days, the total amount of nonexistent funds deposited at both banks is $1,450. On January 5, there will be a balance of $350 in one account and $550 in the other. The kiter may then withdraw all of the money from both accounts and hit the road.

In some cases the kiter intends to, and does, make good on the checks he writes. His purpose may be to float his checks between banks, thus giving himself a sort of interest-free loan.

*   *   *

Roger Lefevre, 25, a Salt Lake City businessman, was convicted in 1983 on charges of felony theft by deception for allegedly stealing hundreds of thousands of dollars from investors in his company, a loan corporation. He pleaded guilty to one count of second-degree felony theft and was put on probation. He has recently been charged with first-degree felony communications fraud and second-degree felony theft for kiting checks.

In the alleged kiting scheme, Lefevre and an associate reportedly floated checks between two business accounts supposedly containing millions of dollars. According to charges, between September 1984 and June 1985, the two passed daily checks averaging $65,000 between accounts.

Lefevere and his partner then allegedly withdrew $347,000 in cash, "which is now owed to the victim, First Interstate Bank, since it was the last bank holding the checks when the fraud fell apart," according to charges.

Money Order Forgery

Since 1981, $5 million in altered money orders have been recovered, according to U.S. Postal Service officials, but it is unknown how many millions are still outstanding. Money-order falsification is one of the easiest types of forgery to master.

A money order is bought in the amount of one or two dollars; the forger uses Liquid Paper or a similar product to obscure the amount and then photocopies the document. Using a check-writing machine, a larger dollar figure is typed in.

The media brought money-order forgery to the attention of the nation in 1985, when a scheme that had been operating out of the Mississippi State Penitentiary at Parchman for at least five years was revealed.

According to George Allred, already serving time for armed robbery when convicted for his part in the scam, money orders in small amounts were obtained from outside the penitentiary. A razor blade was used to scrape off the original amounts, and then a typewriter or black ballpoint pen was used to fill in larger amounts, usually $500. (Allred explained to a federal court jury that his skill at this varied, depending upon whether he was drunk or sober.)

Another step in the scam was to recruit people from outside the prison to cash the checks. This was done by placing ads in pen-pal magazines, among them *Cupid's Destiny.* "Lonely man doing lonely time" was how Allred said he prefaced his ads. Usually gay men and elderly women responded.

After a friendship was formed through letter-writing, inmates would ask "pen pals" to cash the $500 money orders, enclosed in a letter. They would be told to spend part of the money on themselves, then forward the rest to accomplices, also outside the prison, for whom addresses were given. The accomplices would split the money with the prisoners.

The pen pals who cashed the money orders did not know that they were fraudulent, according to testimony, but are held accountable for paying them off. In some cases the amounts to be paid back are as high as $5,000.

It is interesting to note, however, that not all of the recipients of the money orders sent the money to the accomplices. Some sent only a fraction of the amount requested; in one case an elderly woman put several thousand dollars in her freezer and spent it slowly on her own bills.

U.S. postal inspectors say that this is the largest U.S. Postal Service money-order fraud ever. There have been about fifty arrests in connection with this scheme during the last five years of inmates, participating guards, and accomplices, and officials say that about fifty more arrests are expected.

Gordon C. Morison, an assistant postmaster general, announced that the Postal Service would revamp money orders due to the alarming increase of altered money orders involving prison inmates. The new money orders, designed to be counterfeit proof, will be printed in pastel colors that are difficult to reproduce, and a chemical treatment will be used on the paper to reveal any attempts at alteration. The Postal Service hopes that the new money orders will be available by mid 1987.

Counterfeiting

Some counterfeiters are so poor at their chosen profession that it's a wonder they ever took up the "art." Bills were discovered in Stuart, Florida, that had been created with a photocopy machine and colored pencils.

"They were sorry looking," commented a law-enforcement officer. Another officer remarked that they were probably only good enough to be passed in a dimly lit room.

Counterfeiters of the "coloring book" type don't worry federal treasury officials too much, but there are some expert craftsmen in this illegal trade that do.

In 1984, counterfeiters nationwide produced almost $90 million in fake currency. With higher-tech machinery available to the criminal, officials fear that the country could soon be flooded with bogus money. Photocopy machines with multicolor capabilities are already within the grasp of the enterprising money-maker.

The best way to tell a good counterfeit bill from real U.S. currency is to lay the suspect bill side by side with a legitimate bill of the same denomination. The real bill should have an appearance of greater depth; it should look more three-dimensional than the fake money. The reason for this is that most counterfeiters use a printing process called photo-offset, while the government uses engraved plates. The engraving process gives the bill its three-dimensional look.

The U.S. Treasury is considering various changes in the American greenback. In years to come, bills may have watermarks like French francs, special security threads, or additional color fibers woven into the paper. Micro-printed plastic or metal threads measuring less than one-sixteenth of an inch in width would be visible in a bill held up to the light, and would be very difficult to duplicate.

Michael F. Murphy, special-agent-in-charge of the Jacksonville, Florida, office of the U.S. Secret Service, an agency of the Treasury Department, has said that counterfeit bills are difficult to detect but, if you are stuck with one, there's not much you can do.

"The person who has a counterfeit bill is like the one who has a bad check," he said. "It's a worthless piece of paper. If they go to the bank and deposit $1,000 and there's a fake twenty-dollar bill in there, the bank won't give them credit for that bill. The public is the one that loses."

Bibliography

"A Pitifully Small Amount," *Journal Courier* (New Haven, CT), September 16, 1985.

"A Shameful Quest for Profits," *Staten Island Advance* (Staten Island, NY), September 20, 1985.

"Action Line," *Sun* (Gainesville, FL), October 6, 1985.

"Activator Supply Fined $320,550," *Record Times* (Wheatland, WY), September 25, 1985.

"Alleged Scheme Milks Investors," by Steve Marble, *Daily Pilot* (Costa Mesa, CA), September 15, 1985.

"Arrest Warrant Issued for Los Banos Palmist," *Sun-Star* (Merced, CA), September 27, 1985.

"Attorney, Clients Indicted in Oil, Gas Operation," *Sun-Tattler* (Hollywood, FL), October 16, 1985.

"Bank Card Scams," *Worcester Telegram* (Worcester, MA), October 3, 1985.

"Bensalem Pair Plead Not Guilty," by Bill Yingling, *Courier Times* (Levittown, PA), September 27, 1985.

"Beware of Culture Growing Schemes," *Crane Chronicle Stone Country Republican* (Crane, MO), September 5, 1985.

"Beware of Dishonest Repair Persons, Gunter Warns Hurricane Victims," *Independent Post* (Live Oak, FL), September 12, 1985.

"Beware of 'Get Rich Quick' Schemes," by Joseph I. Lieberman, *Suburban News* (Shelton, CT), September 26, 1985.

"Beware of Insurance Scam," by J.P. Tremblay, *News-Press* (Glendale, CA), September 28, 1985.

"Bogus Project Case Ruling Faces Appeal, *Times Record* (Troy, NY), September 20, 1985.

"Bondsman Captures Home Remodeler Holed Up in Claiborne County Closet," by Leslie Henderson, *Journal* (Knoxville, TN), September 21, 1985.

"Broward Man Held on Fraud Charge," *Miami News* (Miami, FL), October 25, 1985.

"Business Bureau Warns of Fraud," *News* (Sidney, OH), October 5, 1985.

"Businessman Was Involved in Fire at Store," by Hurst Laviana, *Eagle and Beacon* (Wichita, KS), October 4, 1985.

"Busting the Bhagwan: Swami of Sex Arrested," by Monroe Anderson and Linda Prout, *Newsweek Magazine*, November 11, 1985.

"Chain Letter Promises Riches, Yields Fraud," by Leslie Henderson, *Journal* (Knoxville, TN), October 31, 1985.

"Charges Brought in Rental-Fraud Scam," *News-Journal* (Pensacola, FL), October 11, 1985.

"Charities and Fraud," *Watertown Daily Times* (Watertown, NY), September 17, 1985.

"Charity Drive is a Fraud, State Charges," by Hal Ellis, *Daily Times* (Primos, PA), October 29, 1985.

"Charity Scam Alleged Ex-Livermore Man Charged," by Mike Myslinski, *Tri-Valley Herald* (Livermore, CA), October 10, 1985.

"Check Fraud Gets Man Five Years," *Gazette* (Stillwater, MN), September 16, 1985.

"Check Legitimacy of Solicitors for Mexican Relief," *Banner* (San Francisco, CA), September 27, 1985.

"Check Scheme Uncovered," *Cumberland and County Times* (Crossville, TN), September 27, 1985.

"Chief Urges Caution After Couple Fleeced," by Nick Martinski, *Review* (Forest Park, IL), October 30, 1985.

"Chiropractor Guilty," *Register Star* (Rockford, IL), October 10, 1985.

"Clever Counterfeiters' Bills Now More Difficult to Detect," by William E. Marden, *Jacksonville Journal* (Jacksonville, FL), October 9, 1985.

"Clovis Man Gets 18-Month Term in Perpetual Motion Stocks Scam," by News-Journal Staff, *News-Journal* (Clovis, NM), September 19, 1985.

"Con Artist Gets Suspended Term," by Harry Harris, *Oakland Tribune* (Oakland, CA), September 16, 1985.

"Con Artists Con Themselves," *South Mississippi Sun* (Biloxi, MS), September 30, 1985.

"Con Artists Conned," *Sun News* (Myrtle Beach, SC), September 30, 1985.

"Con Artists Here Again," by Amy Todd Geisel, *Knoxville News-Sentinel* (Knoxville, TN), October 11, 1985.

"Con Artists Hit Farmers," *Reflex* (Buffalo, MO), October 23, 1985.

"Con Artists Sell False Hopes," *News* (St. John, KS), September 18, 1985.

"Con Artists Swindle Shopper," by Julie Gilberto, *News and Record* (Greensboro, NC), September 20, 1985.

"Con Man Gets $1,800 in Phony-Deposit Scam," *Herald* (Everett, WA), September 17, 1985.

"Con Man Who Posed As Doctor Gets 18 Months For Robbing Family," by Scott Shane, *Sun* (Baltimore, MD), October 3, 1985.

"Con Man's Victim Put Drug Team in Jeopardy," by Cassie Macduff, *Enterprise* (Davis, CA), October 18, 1985.

"Con Men Prey on Farmers," *Sun* (Winchester, KY), October 8, 1985.

"Con Men Selling Fake Repair Jobs," by James Coburn, *Express-News* (San Antonio, TX), September 28, 1985.

"Con Suspect: 'I Needed Drug Money'," by Bob Levenson, *Sentinel* (Orlando, FL), September 15, 1985.

"Cons Goof, Elderly Victim Ends Up with $1,300," *Poughkeepsie-Journal* (Poughkeepsie, NY), September 30, 1985.

"Consumer Corner," by Kevin Wright, *News* (Ulysses, KS), September 26, 1985.

"Consumer Protection for Farmers," *Independent* (Oskaloosa, KS), September 19, 1985.

"Consumers Alerted to Candy Hustle," *Phoenix Log* (Seward, AK), October 3, 1985.

"Controlling Charities," *Herald* (New Britain, CT), October 14, 1985.

"Convicted Con Man Goes on Trial," *Review-Journal* (Las Vegas, NV), October 1, 1985.

"Countians Indicted for Fraud," *McCurtain Gazette* (Idabel, OK), September 27, 1985.

"Country Charmer Ran Slick Con," by Ford Risley, *Florida Times-Union* (Jacksonville, FL), October 21, 1985.

"Couple Arraigned on Fraud Charge," by Jay E. Nachman, *Times Herald* (Norristown, PA), September 27, 1985.

"Couple Claims New Account Not Accurate," by John Lovejoy, *Daily Ledger-Post Dispatch* (Antioch, CA), September 29, 1985.

"Court Orders Shark Hoax Teen Held," by Christine Cocoves, *News* (Stuart, FL), October 3, 1985.

"Court Prepares to Hand Out Culture Farms Funds," by Katherine Weickert, *Journal-World* (Lawrence, KS), September 14, 1985.

"Court Returns Indictment," *Citizen* (Baxter Springs, KS), September 19, 1985.

"Coventry Man Charged with Sports-Car Scams," by Scott Mackay and Bob Mell, *Evening Bulletin* (Providence, RI), September 26, 1985.

"Cracking Down on Pyramid Schemes," by Mary Leidig, *Times-News* (Kingsport, TN), September 22, 1985.

"Crawford Pleads Guilty to Fraud," by Joe Layden, *Journal* (Flat River, MO), September 12, 1985.

"Credit Card Fraud Plagues Businesses," by Jay D. Evensen, *Review-Journal* (Las Vegas, NV), October 21, 1985.

"Credit-Card Phone Fraud Grows in U.S.," by Leon E. Wynter, *Asian Wall Street Journal* (New York, NY), September 27, 1985.

"Culture Farms Officials Fear Charges They Face," by Caroline Trowbridge, *Journal-World* (Lawrence, KS), September 20, 1985.

"D.A. Probes Handyman Scam," by Albert Jimenez, *Daily Item* (Port Chester, NY), September 26, 1985.

"Defrauder Cheated Ailing Man of $6,000," by Betsy Lumbye, *Sun* (Colorado Springs, CO), October 12, 1985.

"Denver Case Link in Vast Credit Fraud," by Ray Flack, *Denver Post* (Denver, CO), October 25, 1983.

"Deputies Charge Greece Resident in Business Deal," *Democrat and Chronicle* (Rochester, NY), October 20, 1985.

"Deputies: Sad Story was a $10,000 Flimflam," by Sandra Mathers, *Sentinel* (Orlando, FL), September 9, 1985.

"Devil Did It! British Man Nets $313,000," by Joseph Lelyveld, *New York Times* (New York, NY), May 4, 1986.

"Don't Let Dream Merchants Smooth Talk You," *Kiowa County Signal* (Greensburg, KS), September 25, 1985.

"Elderly Man Loses Money in Check Scam," *News* (Goshen, IN), October 11, 1985.

"Elderly Monticello Woman Con Artists' Victim," by Charlie Crist, *Democrat* (Callicoon, NY), September 27, 1985.

"Elderly Woman Bilked Out of $8,500 in Savings," *Fresno Bee* (Fresno, CA), September 16, 1985.

"Ex-Con Artist," by David Horst, *Post-Crescent* (Appleton, WI), October 24, 1985.

"Ex-Fireman Sentenced in Car Accident Fraud," by Linnet Myers, *Chicago Tribune* (Chicago, IL), October 2, 1985.

"Ex-Girlfriend Says Shark Attack Hoax 'Wasted Good Life'," by Jim Reeder, *Palm Beach Post* (West Palm Beach, FL), September 25, 1985.

"Families Burned by Rent Scam," by Bill Dingwall, *News-Journal* (Pensacola, FL), October 7 1985.

"Farewell to Rancho Rajneesh," *Time Magazine,* December 9, 1985.

"Farmers Warned About Advance Fee Loan Racket," *Gazette Record* (St. Maries, ID), October 16, 1985.

"FBI Agent Crosses Line into Crime," by M. Anthony Lednovich, *Fort Lauderdale News* (Fort Lauderdale, FL), October 7, 1985.

"FBI Arrests 35 Black Hebrews," *New York Times* (New York, NY), July 17, 1985.

"FBI Nabs 3 on Charges of Credit-Card Fraud," by Gregg Laskoski, *Daily Argus* (Mount Vernon, NY), September 9, 1985.

"Federal Panel Indicts Pair in Fraud Case," *Union* (Sacramento, CA), September 21, 1985.

"Fertilizer Fraud Case Cracked," by Michael Sallah, *News* (Boca Raton, FL), October 24, 1985.

"Fertilizer Fraud Charged," by Staff and Wire Reports, *Miami Herald* (Miami, FL), October 24, 1985.

"Financial Planners Continue Unregulated," *Changing Times, Kiplinger Herald* (Austin, MN), September 15, 1985.

"Fisherman Doesn't Bite," by Tim Roberts, *Daily Ledger and Post Dispatch* (Antioch, CA), October 5, 1985.

"Five Convicted in Money-Order Scam," by Mary Dixon, *Clarion-Ledger* (Jackson, MS), October 9, 1985.

"Five-O Star Takes the Stand in Rewald Trial," *Milwaukee Sentinel* (Milwaukee, WI), September 12, 1985.

"Flim Flam Reported," *Times* (Valdosta, GA), October 21, 1985

"Former Valley Resident Arrested with Rajneesh," *News* (Indio, CA), October 31, 1985.

"Four Accused of Fraud," *Poughkeepsie-Journal* (Poughkeepsie, NY), September 24, 1985.

"Four in Salem Accused of Bilking Woman," *Times & World News* (Roanoke, VA), October 15, 1985.

"Four Indicted in Farm Fraud," *Commercial News* (Danville, IL), October 12, 1985.

"Fraud Suspect Will Be Tried in Vero Beach," by Larry Reisman, *Press Journal* (Vero Beach, FL), October 25, 1985.

"Fraud Suspect: $2 Million in Securities Stolen," by David Uhler, *Fort Lauderdale News* (Fort Lauderdale, FL), October 3, 1985.

"Fraud Suspected: 'Wish' Volunteers Investigate," *Fort Worth Star-Telegram* (Fort Worth, TX), October 5, 1985.

"From Tax Whiz to State Prisoner," by Roger Roy, *Sentinel* (Orlando, FL), October 6, 1985.

"Fulton Sleuth Tracks Flim Flam Artists with Keen Scent for Scam," by James Alexander, Jr., *Record* (Gibson, GA), October 4, 1985.

"Fund for Charity Could Be Fraud," by Robin Bulman, *Gazette* (Billings, MT), September 21, 1985.

"Get-Rich-Quick Deal Just a Pot of Mold," *Newsweek Magazine*, August 19, 1985.

"Gibbon Minister Charged with Theft by Swindle," *Enterprise* (Glencoe, MN), September 19, 1985.

"Gibbon Minister Pleads Guilty," *News Herald* (Le Sueur, MN), October 7, 1985.

"Gibbon Pastor Charged in Theft Case," *News* (Winthrop, MN), September 17, 1985.

"Give a Child Xmas Cancels Solicitation," *Saratogian* (Saratoga Springs, NY), October 24, 1985.

"Givers Beware," *Register* (New Haven, CT), September 16, 1985.

"Good Cause Gone Wrong," *Herald* (New Britain, CT), September 17, 1985.

"Grand Jury Indicts 4 More in Insurance Fraud Case," by Anne Carothers-Kay, *The Des Moines Register* (Des Moines, IA), October 25, 1985.

"Guilty in Hawaii Fraud Case," *New York Times* (New York, NY), October 22, 1985.

"Guilty Plea Heard in Car Scam," *Freeman* (Kingston, NY), October 6, 1985.

"Gypsy Allegedly Casts Evil Spell," by Greg Fieg-Pizano, *Times* (Corpus Christi, TX), October 3, 1985.

"Hapless Victims," by Wendy L. Wall, *Wall Street Journal* (New York, NY), August 13, 1985.

"Hartigan Files Fraud Suit," *Mount Greenwood Express*, October 10, 1985.

"HB Man Sentenced for Energy Scheme," *Daily Pilot* (Costa Mesa, CA), October 19, 1985.

"He Gained Their Trust, Money—and They Wait for Payoff," *Daily Herald,* (Barrington, IL), September 30, 1985.

"Hearing Set for Luddens," *Ledger* (Antioch, CA), October 29, 1985.

"Herbicide Quacks' Hawking May Leave Mess," *Waterfront* (Lake City, MI), September 11, 1985.

"Hoax Suspect Waives Extradition," by Jim Reeder, *Palm Beach Post* (West Palm Beach, FL), September 27, 1985.

"Homeowners Get Warning on Con Men," *Hour* (Norwalk, CT), October 15, 1985.

"How Loan Scam's Architect Charmed, Then Bilked Iowans," by Nick Lamberto, *Des Moines Register* (Des Moines, IA), October 6, 1985.

"How You Can Spot Phony Charities," *Sunday Times* (Primos, PA), September 15, 1985.

ICPI Report, Insurance Crime Prevention Institute, October/December 1983.

"Impostors Undercut Wish Granters' Work," by Elizabeth Simpson, *Fort Worth Star-Telegram* (Fort Worth, TX), October 11, 1985.

"Indiana Inmates Involved in Money Order Swindle," *Times* (Brazil, IN), September 19, 1985.

"Indicted for Mail Fraud," *Sentinel Republican* (Lincoln, KS), September 19, 1985.

"Indictment Charges Three in Phony Mining Scam," by Prentice Palmer, *Atlanta Constitution* (Atlanta, GA), September 18, 1985.

"Indictments Filed on Largest Mail Fraud Pyramid Scheme in History," by Kevin Kelly, *Johnson County Sun* (Shawnee Mission, KS), September 13, 1985.

"Indictments Issued in Culture-Growing Scheme," by Mede Nix, *Monitor-Index and Democrat* (Moberly, MO), September 12, 1985.

"Inmate Guilty in Scam," *Island Packet* (Hilton Head Island, SC), September 25, 1985.

"Inmate Tries to Take Blame in Postal Scam," by Mary Dixon, *Clarion-Ledger* (Jackson, MS), October 8, 1985.

"Insurance Agent Charged with Bilking Widow," *Schenectady Gazette* (Schenectady, NY), September 24, 1985.

"Insurance Fraud Trial Under Way," *Peoria Journal Star* (Peoria, IL), October 23, 1985.

"Insurance Fraud Trial Under Way," by Patricia Elich, *Sun-Sentinel* (Ft. Lauderdale, FL), October 23, 1985.

"Insurer Has History of Fraud Suits," by Stan Jones, *Fort Worth Star-Telegram* (Fort Worth, TX), September 20, 1985 (Eve.).

"Investigator Charges 2 with Fraud in Check Kiting," by Mike Carter, *Salt Lake Tribune* (Salt Lake City, UT), October 10, 1985.

"Investment Advisers May Be Conmen in Disguise, Bureau Warns," *Chronicle* (Hamden, CT), October 9, 1985.

"Investment Advisers may be Common in Disguise, Bureau Warns," *Chronicle* (Hamden, CT), October 9, 1985.

"Investment Counselor Guilty of Fraud," *Tacoma News Tribune* (Tacoma, WA), October 22, 1985.

"Israel Asks Us to Take Back Black Muslims," *New York Times* (New York, NY), April 15, 1985.

"It's Easy to Chew Up Logic," by Ron Wiggins, *Palm Beach Post* (West Palm Beach, FL), September 12, 1985.

"Iuka Residents Named in Postal Scam Trial," by Staff and Wire Reports, *Corinthian* (Corinth, MS), October 3, 1985.

"Jail Puts Bite on Stuart Teen's Shark Hoax," by Jim Reeder, *Palm Beach Post* (West Palm Beach, FL), September 8, 1985.

"Judge Rules Mistrial in Insurance Case," *Miami Herald* (Miami, FL), October 26, 1985.

"Jurors Consider Case of Magic at Local Bar," by Rosanne Pagano, *Times* (Anchorage, Alaska), October 18, 1985.

"Jury Acquits Con Man on Charges of Conspiracy," *Review-Journal* (Las Vegas, NV), October 8, 1985.

"Jury Acquits Perry," *Nevada Appeal* (Carson City, NV), October 8, 1985.

"Kinster Still Considers Justice a Good Friend," by Christine Cocoves, *News* (Stuart, FL), October 3, 1985.

"Knutson Free on $2,000 Bond," *New Record* (Gillete, WY), September 25, 1985.

"La Jolla Woman, 97, Awarded $2 Million in Fraud," *Light* (La Jolla, CA), October 10, 1985.

"Landrum Couple Fall Victim to Painting Flim-Flam Scheme," by Jody Raines, *News Leader* (Landrum, SC), October 10, 1985.

"Larceny Charge," *Times Record* (Troy, NY), September 24, 1985.

"Lawmen Arrest 3 in Fake Money Scheme," by Mike Bucsko, *News* (Stuart, FL), October 10, 1985.

"Lawyer Jailed in $957,000 Swindle," *Near North News* (Chicago, IL), October 12, 1985.

"Lena Elmendorf Pleads Guilty," *Townsman* (Hyde Park, NY), October 2, 1985.

"Local Businesses Conned by Magazine Scam," by Angela Tierney, *Bayou Times* (Crestview, FL), September 25, 1985.

"Locals 'Taken' in Nationwide Credit Scam," by Peggy Edwards, *Pasco News* (Dade City, FL), August 23, 1985.

"Lower Than Low," *News* (Naugatuck, CT), September 18, 1985.

"Man Accused of Soliciting for Lawyer," by Christina Cheakalos, *Miami Herald* (Miami, FL), October 26, 1985.

"Man Arrested for Lost-Pet Extortion Scam," by Clem Richardson and Larry Cose, *Chicago Sun-Times* (Chicago, IL), September 25, 1985.

"Man Assessed Prison Term in Stolen Check Scam," *Houston Chronicle* (Houston, TX), October 4, 1985.

"Man Avoids being Victim of Con Artists," *Times* (Pekin, IL), October 10, 1985.

"Man Called Master 'Con Artist' Nabbed by Police," by Jean Saile, *Oakland Press* (Pontiac, MI), October 18, 1985.

"Man Charged in Fake Kidnapping Scam," by Jeff Mangum, *Tampa Tribune* (Tampa, FL), October 4, 1985.

"Man Enters Plea in Seward Fraud Scheme," by Dirk Miller, *Peninsula Clarion* (Kenai, AK), October 17, 1985.

"Man Faces Fraud Charges," *Sun-Tattler* (Hollywood, FL), October 25, 1985.

"Man Gets Jail Term in Lost Pet Scam," by Jim Casey, *Chicago Sun-Times* (Chicago, IL), October 19, 1985.

"Man Loses $500 in Scam," *Savannah Evening Press* (Savannah, GA), September 19, 1985.

"Man Sentenced in Counterfeiting," by Mickie Valente, *Jacksonville Journal* (Jacksonville, FL), October 1, 1985.

"Man Who Faked Disability," *Post-Bulletin* (Rochester, MN), September 13, 1985.

"Man With Hard-Luck Tale Faces More Theft Charges," by Prakash Gandhi, *Sentinel* (Orlando, FL), September 26, 1985.

"Man's Credit Folds with Theft of Wallet," by John Brady, *Atlanta Journal* (Atlanta, GA), September 16, 1985.

"Manager of Garrison Distict Innocent till Proven Guilty," *Journal* (Devils Lake, ND), September 20, 1985.

"Meals on Wheels Fund Solicitors are Called Bogus," *Register Pajaronian* (Watsonville, CA), September 14, 1985.

"Merchants Warned about Bad Checks," *Chronicle* (Crossville, TN), September 27, 1985.

"Milk-Culture Firms Told to Pay $320,550," *Wyoming State Tribune* (Cheyenne, WY), September 21, 1985.

"MS Victim's Lawyer Gets 7 Years," by Don Hayner, *Chicago Sun-Times* (Chicago, IL), October 8, 1985.

"My Wife Meets Two Con-Game Women at the Mall," by Curtis Bigelow, *Newsday* (Garden City, NY), October 6, 1985.

"Mystic Charged with Exorcising Cash, Jewelry," by Bill Cotteral, *Democrat* (Tallahassee, FL), October 17, 1985.

"Newspaper Ad Leads to Arrest for Bilking Merchants," *Star-Tribune* (Casper, WY), October 18, 1985.

"Officer Delivers Woe for a Fraud Suspect," by Joel Silverman, *Virginian-Pilot* (Norfolk, VA), October 24, 1985.

"Officers Confiscate Fair Booths Items," *Holmes County Advertiser* (Bonifay, FL), October 2, 1985.

"Officials to Decide on Fund to Repay Culture Investors," by Michael Ryan, *Capital-Journal* (Topeka, KS), September 17, 1985.

"Old Con Backfires," *Herald* (Bradenton, FL), September 30, 1985.

"Owner of Defunct Fertilizer Plant is Accused," by Rich Pollack, *Fort Lauderdale News* (Fort Lauderdale, FL), October 24, 1985.

"Pair Helps Woman Cross Street, Robs Her," *Daily Camera* (Boulder, CO), July 6, 1985.

"Palm Reader Accused in Scam," *Corpus Christi Caller* (Corpus Christi, TX), October 4, 1985.

"Parchman Guards Sentenced for Fraud," *Journal* (Tupelo, MS), October 4, 1985.

"Pastor Charged With Theft," *Journal* (New Ulm, MN), September 13, 1985.

"Patrolman Indicted in Fraud Case," by Michael Pearson, *Light* (San Antonio, TX), September 25, 1985.

"People. Explanation," *New York Times Large Type Weekly* (New York, NY), September 23, 1985.

"Phone Fraud: Latest Scam in Credit Cards," by Leon F. Wynter, *Wall Street Journal* (Brussels, Belgium), September 11, 1985.

"Picking Jury May Be Slow in Fraud Case," from staff reports, *Sentinel* (Orlando, FL), October 8, 1985.

"Plans Unfolding to Foil Future Counterfeiters," by Roger Boye, *Chicago Tribune* (Chicago, IL), October 6, 1985.

"Plastic Perpetrators," by Rick Griffin, *National Centurion Magazine,* November 1983.

"Police Arrest Man for Charity Scam," *Star-Tribune* (Casper, WY), October 17, 1985.

"Police Arrest Phony Solicitor," *Sun Herald* (Cleveland, OH), October 3, 1985.

"Police Having Spell over Witch Doctor Rape Case," by Stanley P. Klevan, *Record* (Stockton, CA), September 27, 1985.

"Police Warn of Con Game Based on Interracial Trust," *Herald* (Everett, WA), September 21, 1985.

"Ponzi Patsies," by Lance Evans, *Times* (Scranton, PA), September 11, 1985.

"Ponzi Schemes Bilk Millions from Naive," by Lynn Phillips, *Sentinel,* (Orlando, FL), October 14, 1985.

"Postal Service to Make Money Orders Counterfeit-Proof," by Mary Dixon, *Clarion Ledger* (Jackson, MS), October 10, 1985.

"Prisoner Says He Tried Scam to Get $1500," *State* (Columbia, SC), September 25, 1985.

"Probe of Charity Focuses on Loans," by Tamara Lytle, *Register* (New Haven, CT), September 19, 1985.

"Professed Faith Healer Arrested on Fraud Charges," by Gregory Wooten, *Gadsden County Times* (Quincy, FL), September 19, 1985.

"Project Collected $13,000 during Summer Fundraiser," by Paul Choiniere, *Bulletin* (Norwick, CT), September 14, 1985.

"'Prophet' Without Honor, Court Says," by Irv Randolph, *Tribune* (Philadelphia, PA), October 25, 1985.

"Prosecution Is Uncertain for Witch Doctor from Stockton," by Paul Feist, *News-Sentinel* (Lodi, CA), September 24, 1985.

"Prosecution Rests: Bankruptcy Controller Says Rewald Ran Scam," by Walter Wright, *Honolulu Advertiser* (Honolulu, HI), October 2, 1985.

"Prosecutor Opposes Bond in Culture Case," *Journal World* (Lawrence, KS), September 24, 1985.

"Protect Your Credit Card," by Stephan Wilkinson, *Travel & Leisure Magazine,* June 1983.

"Protecting Charities against Fraud," by State Sen. M. Adela Eads, *Journal* (Lakeville, CT), October 10, 1985.

"PSL Teen Charged in Hoax," by Mike Bucsko, *News* (Stuart, FL), October 12, 1985.

"Psychic Expected to Give Herself Up," by Warren Williams, *Bee* (Modesto, CA), October 25, 1985.

"Quiz Traps Illegal Immigrants," *Missoulian* (Missoula, MT), October 28, 1985,

"Racing Meet Draws Con Artists to Lexington, Police Say," by Valarie Honeycutt, *Herald-Leader* (Lexington, KY), October 14, 1985.

"Rajneeshis Regroup after Exodus of Top Officials," by Rogers Worthington, *Chicago Tribune* (Chicago, IL), September 22, 1985.

"Receptionists Targets of Scam," by France Griggs, *Cincinnati Post* (Cincinnati, OH), October 11, 1985.

"Red Cross Warns of Solicitations," *Post* (Paradise, CA), October 4, 1985.

"Restaurant Writer under Investigation," by Patricia Sullivan, *Missoulian* (Missoula, MT), September 19, 1985.

"Restraint against Feelin' Inc.," by Kris Radish, *Deseret News* (Salt Lake City, UT), September 19, 1985.

"Retail Crime; The Pen is Mightier Than the Gun," by Nancy Rutter, *Island Packet* (Hilton Head Island, SC), October 25, 1985.

"Rewald Business Ties Denied by TV Star," *Milwaukee Journal* (Milwaukee, WI), September 12, 1985.

"Rewald Is not Likely to Testify for Himself," *Milwaukee Sentinel* (Milwaukee, WI), October 9, 1985.

"Rondout Wheeler-Dealer Tries to Jump Bail," by Tom Wakeman, *Freeman* (Kingston, NY), October 20, 1985.

"Roopville Woman is Flim-Flam Victim," *Daily Times Georgian* (Carrollton, GA), October 25, 1985.

"S. L. Man Ordered to Halt Property Sales," *Deseret News* (Salt Lake City, UT), October 2, 1985.

"Salesman Surrenders in Gallatin," by Charlie Appleton, *Nashville Banner* (Nashville, TN), October 15, 1985.

"Scam Operation is Conducted to Steal Secretaries' Purses," *News-Register* (Wheeling, WV), September 29, 1985.

"Scam, Says Rewald Company Trustee," by Charles Memminger, *Honolulu Star-Bulletin* (Honolulu, HI), October 2, 1985.

"Scams, Too, Play a Role in Efforts to Find Missing Children," by Debby McDonald, *Johnson County Sun* (Shawnee Mission, KS), October 9, 1985.

"Self-Help Plan Must Pay, Claims State," by Joan O'Brien, *Salt Lake Tribune* (Salt Lake City, UT), October 11, 1985.

"Sentence Due on 20th Attempt," by John Melson, *News-Press* (Glendale, CA), September 21, 1985.

"Shark Fraud Youth Found," *Telegraphy Herald* (Dubuque, IA), September 25, 1985.

"Shark Hoax Suspect Arrested," by Bernie Woodall, *News Tribune* (Fort Pierce, FL), September 24, 1985.

"Shark Hoax Suspect Due," *News Tribune* (Fort Pierce, FL), October 1, 1985.

"Shark Hoax Suspect Faces Extradition," by Sue Smith, *News Tribune* (Fort Pierce, FL), September 25, 1985.

"Shark Hoax Suspect in Court Today," by Ann McCallum, *News Tribune* (Fort Pierce, FL), October 2, 1985.

"Shark-Hoax Suspect to be Tried as Adult," by Ann McCallum, *News Tribune* (Fort Pierce, FL), September 26, 1985.

"Shark Hoax Teen Returns from L.A.," by Mike Bucsko, *News* (Stuart, FL), October 2, 1985.

"Sheela Strikes Back," *Newsweek Magazine* (NY), October 7, 1985.

"Shortchange Artist Sought," *Journal* (Franklin, IN), October 11, 1985.

"State Accuses City Charity," by Greg Mizera, *Waterbury Republican* (Waterbury, CT), September 13, 1985.

"State Attorney General Scored on Remarks," *Waterbury Republican* (Waterbury, CT), October 5, 1985.

"State Fights to Keep Control of Fraud Case," by Jane Martin, *Fort Worth Star-Telegram* (Fort Worth, TX), September 24, 1985.

"State Queries Fund Raisers' Fees," by Don Schiller, *Record Journal* (Meriden, CT), October 6, 1985.

"State Targets Genie Project," *Waterbury American* (Waterbury, CT), September 13, 1985.

"State Warns against Unclaimed Funds Solicitation Firm," *Sun* (Las Vegas, NV), October 25, 1985.

"State Warns of Pyramid Scemes," *Chronicle* (Camden, TN), October 2, 1985.

"Suit Alleges Falsity in Raising Funds," *Oregonian* (Portland, OR), October 19, 1985.

"Suit Seeks Recovery of Money Paid to Feelin' Great," by K. Radish and V. Schulthies, *Deseret News* (Salt Lake City, UT), October 11, 1985.

"Suspect in Area Gold Scheme Gets Prison Term in California," by Katie Springer, *Sun-Sentinel* (Ft. Lauderdale, FL), September 11, 1985.

"Suspect in Gold Scheme Gets Prison in California," by Katie Springer, *Fort Lauderdale News* (Fort Lauderdale, FL), September 11, 1985.

"Swindle of Widow Headed Off at the Bank," by Joseph Palmer, *Herald* (Bradenton, FL), September 27, 1985.

"Swindler Gets 10-Year Term," by Mark Obbie, *Houston Post* (Houston, TX), October 4, 1985.

"TBI Explores New Charges against Insurance Agent," by Charlie Appleton, *Nashville Banner* (Nashville, TN), October 31, 1985.

"Teen Arrested in Credit Card Scam," by Anthony P. Spinelli and J. D. Shay, *Bridgeport Telegram* (Bridgeport, CT), October 25, 1985.

"Teen Arrested on Theft, Forgery Charges," by River Parishes Bureau, *Morning Advocate* (Baton Rouge, LA), October 19, 1985.

"Texas Man Guilty in Mail Scam," by Lovell Beaulieu, *Times-Picayune States-Item* (New Orleans, LA), October 18, 1985.

"The Billion-Dollar Plastic Hold-Up," by Scott Eyman, *Cleveland Magazine,* June 1983.

"The Con Man," by Bill Boyd, *Telegraph and News* (Macon, GA), October 21, 1985.

"The Return of Arturo Hoyo," by John Dorschner, *Miami Herald* (Miami, FL), October 13, 1985.

"Theft Charges Filed against Gibbon Pastor," *Hub* (Gaylord, MN), September 19, 1985.

"Third Youth is Charged in Weston Credit Scam," by Mark Seavy, *Hour* (Norwalk, CT), October 25, 1985.

"Thirty-Two Black Hebrews Indicted for Fraud," *Chicago Tribune* (Chicago, IL), September 15, 1985.

"Thirty-Two Black Hebrews Indicted for Fraud," *Afro-American* (Baltimore, MD), September 21, 1985.

"This Con Man Pulls Swindles in Yiddish," by Ron Csillag, *Canadian Jewish News* (Toronto, Canada), August 15, 1985.

"Thomson Enters Judgement against Corporations [SIC]," *Rocket Miner* (Rock Springs, WY), September 21, 1985.

"Three Accused of Selling Phony Oil Leases," by Constance Prater, *Miami Herald* (Miami, FL), October 16, 1985.

"Three Arrested for Fraud in Lease Scam," by UPI, *News* (Anchorage, AK), October 16, 1985.

"Three Former Guards Sentenced," *Clarion-Ledger* (Jackson, MS), October 3, 1985.

"Three Held for Fraud," *Bee* (Modesto, CA), October 16, 1985.

"Three Indicted in Credit Card Scheme, by Eric Nagourney, *Herald Statesman* (Yonkers, NY), September 14, 1985.

"Three Indicted in Faked Credit Purchases," by Pam McClintock, *Washington Times* (Washington, D.C.), October 8, 1985.

"Three May Have Seen Spot as Haven," by Michele Derus, *Milwaukee Sentinel* (Milwaukee, WI), September 12, 1985.

"Trial on Bribery Charge Starts for Former Preacher," by Roger Roy, *Sentinel* (Orlando, FL), October 8, 1985.

"Trial Set on Ex-Fayette Man's Mail Fraud Charges," *Register Herald* (Beckley, WV), October 8, 1985.

"Trickster Gets 6 Years for Forgery, Theft Scams," by Paul Langner, *Boston Globe* (Boston, MA), October 20, 1985.

"Twelve Charged with Fraud," *Pioneer* (Johnson, KS), September 19, 1985.

"Twelve Indicted in Sale of Culture Kits," by Ellen Schechet, *Eagle and Beacon* (Wichita, KS), September 12, 1985.

"Twentieth Century Outlaws Go for Plastic Booty," by Tony Sin, *Press* (Vista, CA), October 8, 1985.

"Twenty-Four Court Delays Later, Sentencing Hearing Begins," by John Melson, *News-Press* (Glendale, CA), October 23, 1985.

"Twenty-One Told not to Market Feelin' Great," by Ken Perkins, *Deseret News* (Salt Lake City, UT), September 26, 1985.

"Twenty-Seven from Lawrence File Claims For Culture Investments," by Caroline Trowbridge, *Journal-World* (Lawrence, KS), September 17, 1985.

"Two Arrested in Counterfeiting Case," *Review Journal* (Las Vegas, NV), October 16, 1985.

"Two Con Artists Distract Clerk, Get $200 Cash," *Recorder* (Conshohocken, PA), October 13, 1985.

"Two Demon Busters Get Busted," by Roger Clinton, *Intelligencer Journal* (Lancaster, PA), October 26, 1985.

"Two Exorcists Tricked by Woman, 70," *New Era* (Lancaster, PA), October 26, 1985.

"Two Insurance Agents Charged with Fraud," by Sue Morgan, *Times-West Virginian* (Fairmont, WV), October 17, 1985.

"Two Investors Testify at Rewald Trial," *Honolulu Star-Bulletin* (Honolulu, HI), September 26, 1985.

"Two Men Arrested in Magazine Scam," *Globe-Times* (Bethlehem, PA), October 2, 1985.

"Two Women Charged with Theft," *Milwaukee Sentinel* (Milwaukee, WI), October 19, 1985.

"Two Women Lose Money in Flimflams," *Herald* (Augusta, GA), October 9, 1985.

"Two Women Reported Posing as Nuns," by Regina Ann Purifico, *Times Herald* (Norristown, PA), October 23, 1985.

"U.S. Tracks Bank's Promoter to Philippines," by Steve Jenning, *Oregonian* (Portland, OR), September 19, 1985.

"Unclaimed Property Firm May Be Scam," by Ed Vogel, *Review-Journal* (Las Vegas, NV), October 24, 1985.

"Vacondo Defendant Claims State Missed Trial Deadline," by Roger Roy, *Sentinel* (Orlando, FL), October 9, 1985.

"Vacondo Witness Says He Helped Take Money," by Roger Roy, *Sentinel* (Orlando, FL), October 22, 1985.

"Vanettens Will Go to Trial in January," *Post-Register* (Idaho Falls, ID), October 31, 1985.

"Vial Plan Cash Drive was Scam, Police Say," by Clair Johnson, *Gazette* (Billings, MT), September 22, 1985.

"Victims: Inmates Used Love Letters in Scams," by Mary Dixon, *Clarion-Ledger* (Jackson, MS), October 2, 1985.

"Warrant Issued for Suspect in Charity Scheme," by John Vanlandingham, *Valley Times* (Pleasanton, CA), October 11, 1985.

"Westlake Dynamics," by Joan Abrams, *Morning Tribune* (Lewiston, ID), October 13, 1985.

"Weston Teens are Charged in Credit Card Scam," by Mark Seavy, *Hour* (Norwalk, CT), October 22, 1985.

"Witch Doctor Case Closed," *Record* (Stockton, CA), September 27, 1985.

"Witch Doctor Will Not Face Charges," by Paul Feist, *News-Sentinel* (Lodi, CA), September 25, 1985.

"Witness Details Insurance Practices," by Stephen J. Hedges, *Miami Herald* (Miami, FL), October 24, 1985.

"Witnesses Want Le Fave in Jail," by Brandon Bailey, *Star-News* (Pasadena, CA), October 22, 1985.

"Wizard Waved Crooked Wand, Investors Claim," by Beth Wilson, *Miami Herald* (Miami, FL), September 15, 1985.

"Woman Arrested After Local Charity Fraud," by Joanne Marez, *Sun* (Bremerton, WA), October 26, 1985.

"Woman Falls Prey to Con Games," *North Jersey Herald News* (Passaic, NJ), October 3, 1985.

"Woman Loses $2,800 in Scam," *Peoria Journal Star* (Peoria, IL), October 13, 1985.

"Woman, 77, Acts Senile to Beat Scam," by Gary Gerhardt, *Rocky Mountain News* (Denver, CO), June 5, 1985.

"Woods Not Guilty of Attempting to Defraud," by Anne Causey, *Blacksburg Christiansburg News Messenger* (Christiansburg, VA), September 22, 1985.

"Zack Gets Four Terms," *Courier* (Connellsville, PA), October 2, 1985.

"Zetex Stock is Illegal," *Banner* (Circle, MT), September 26, 1985.

Index